Best Wishes
to Joe Michalek !
+ Happy Travels !
EARL
THOLLANDER
1984

Earl Thollander's
Back Roads of California

Store and Post Office,
Plumas County

Folk art sketched near Cazadero (Oredazac spelled backward), Sonoma County

Earl Thollander's
Back Roads of California

Clarkson N. Potter, Inc./Publishers NEW YORK

DISTRIBUTED BY CROWN PUBLISHERS, INC.

to dear friends
Bill and Barbara

Bush
Penstemon,
Santa Clara County

Published by Clarkson N. Potter, Inc., One Park
Avenue, New York, New York 10016, and simultaneously
in Canada by General Publishing Company Limited

Manufactured in the United States of America

Library of Congress Cataloging in Publication Data

Thollander, Earl.
    Earl Thollander's back roads of California.

    1. California—Description and travel—1981—Guide-
books.   2. Automobiles—Road guides—California.
I. Title.   II. Title: Back roads of California.
F859.3.T525 1983   917.94′0453   82-22461
ISBN 0-517-54966-2 (cloth)
ISBN 0-517-54967-0 (paper)

10 9 8 7 6 5 4 3 2 1

First Edition

Contents

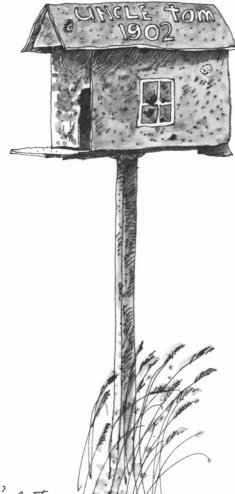

Rural mailbox,
Knoxville Road, Napa County

Central California

Map legend

.___5.6___. distance in miles
between dots

→ → → my route (which may
be reversed should
you desire)

▲ campgrounds
■ towns and cities
▱ dams
‒ ‒ ‒ lake boundaries
‒.‒.‒ trails
.... rivers
□ special place
✕ my sketching place
⌂ church
⊼ picnic grounds
⊞ cemetery
△ mountains
⌂ buildings

NORTH is always toward the
top of the page

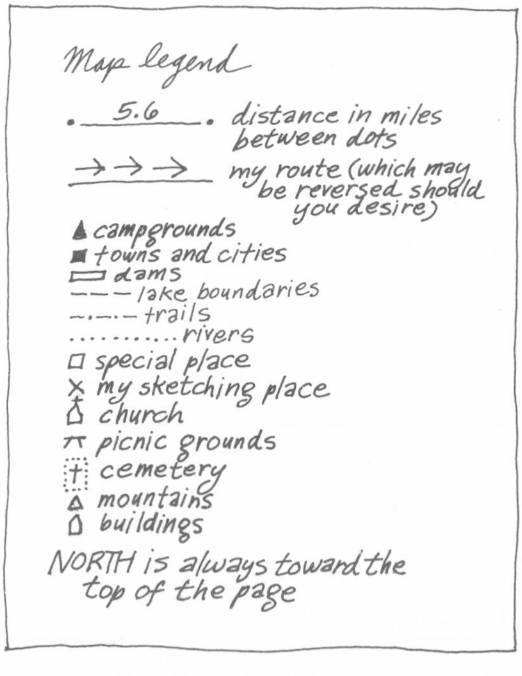

Southern California

napa county

I am grateful to the artist Joe Seney for his good companionship on many of these back road journeys.

Turkey Buzzard,
Stanislaus County

Preface

Earl Thollander's *Back Roads of California* is a nonhighway travel guide to out of the way places. A sequel to the first *Back Roads of California* published more than a decade ago, this new volume augments it to make a more complete guide to areas throughout California. The trips included are as beautiful and as interesting as those in the first volume.

Each of the book's four parts begins with a sectional map. These will help you locate the back roads on larger maps that are available from many sources, including travel services, chambers of commerce, gas stations, tourist bureaus, and automobile clubs. Localized maps for all roads throughout the book will guide you on specific trips. Arrows trace my direction of travel, although the routes can easily be reversed. The North Pole is toward the top of the page. Maps are not to scale because the roads are of varying lengths; however, the mileage notations will provide a sense of their distance.

Your odometer will not measure distance exactly the same as mine, but the differences should not be too great. AAA county and regional maps were essential to me in following the back roads. I also purchased maps at ranger stations when entering forest preserves.

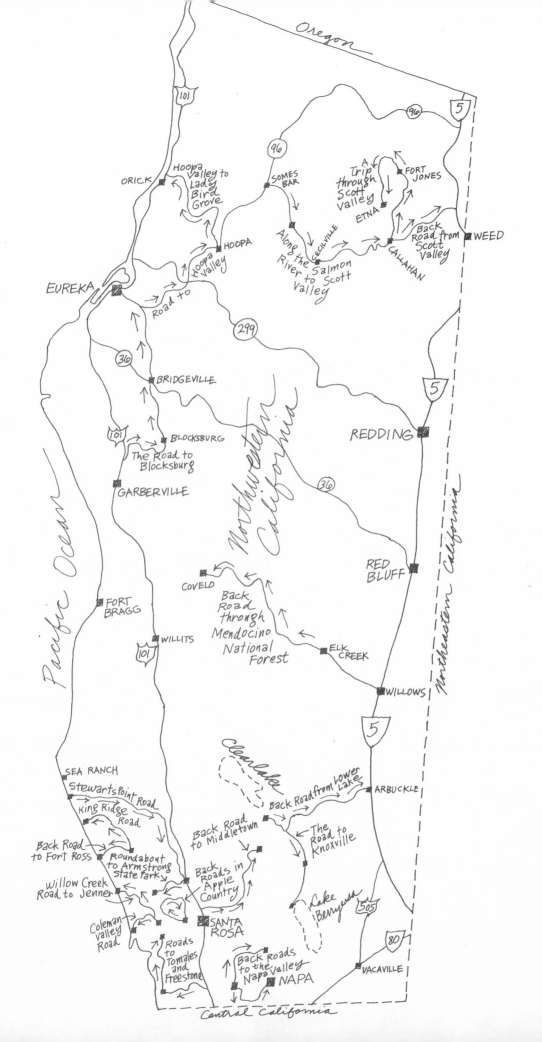

Oregon

101

96

ORICK Hoopa
Valley to
Lady
Bird
Grove

SOMES BAR

A Trip through Scott Valley

FORT JONES

WEED

Along the Salmon River to Scott Valley

CECILVILLE

ETNA

Back Road from Scott Valley

CALLAHAN

HOOPA Hoopa Valley

EUREKA Road to

299

36

BRIDGEVILLE

101 BLOCKSBURG
The Road to Blocksburg

REDDING

GARBERVILLE

Northwestern California

36

Pacific Ocean

COVELD

Back Road Through Mendocino National Forest

RED BLUFF

FORT BRAGG

WILLITS

101

ELK CREEK

WILLOWS

Northeastern California

5

SEA RANCH
Stewarts Point Road
King Ridge Road

Clear Lake

Back Road from Lower Lake

ARBUCKLE

Back Road to Middletown

The Road to Knoxville

Back Road to Fort Ross
Roundabout to Armstrong State Park

Back Roads in Apple Country

Willow Creek Road to Jenner

Lake Berryessa

505

Coleman Valley Road

SANTA ROSA

80

Roads to Tomales and Freestone

Back Roads to the Napa Valley

NAPA

VACAVILLE

Central California

10

I've heard people boast of how fast they went somewhere and how many miles were covered in the time. In the pages that follow there are mountain and coastal roads to enjoy with no regard for speed or the hour.

I start early and let the day unfold. I don't push to get anywhere because I know that the fun and beauty of the back road experience is in the trip itself.

I hesitate to divulge certain roads, but it would be unrealistic to believe they can be saved from change by hiding them. Only for a while, perhaps. And, of course, they are not secret. They are public roads and are catalogued on county maps.

Better to announce their charm and beauty and alert everyone interested to guard against infringements upon them. I also like to think that back road travelers like myself will not drop trash or create disturbances along the way.

Those who live on the back roads and we who enjoy traveling them must be concerned that they remain unspoiled as long as possible.

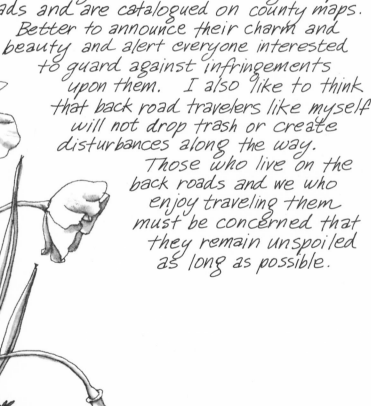

California Poppy, Tehama County

Roads to Tomales and Freestone

Rolling pastureland, cows, old farms, leaning barns, and rows of eucalyptus distinguish this area of California.   I sketch along Carmody Road with a meadowlark's song in the still morning air.
    Curious cows peer at me, then go back to munching the green grass.
    The village of Tomales was established at the head of Keyes Creek with the opening of a store there in 1852. Tomales made its first rail shipment of produce to Sausalito — via the North Pacific Coast Railroad — in 1874, when 300 sacks of potatoes were delivered to be ferried across the Golden Gate to San Francisco.

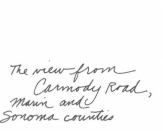

The view from Carmody Road, Marin and Sonoma counties

I sketch the town from across the hills, then drive to nearby Dillon Beach overlooking Bodega Bay. The bay was named by its discoverer, Juan Francisco de la Bodega y Cuadro, in 1775.

The village of Tomales, Marin County

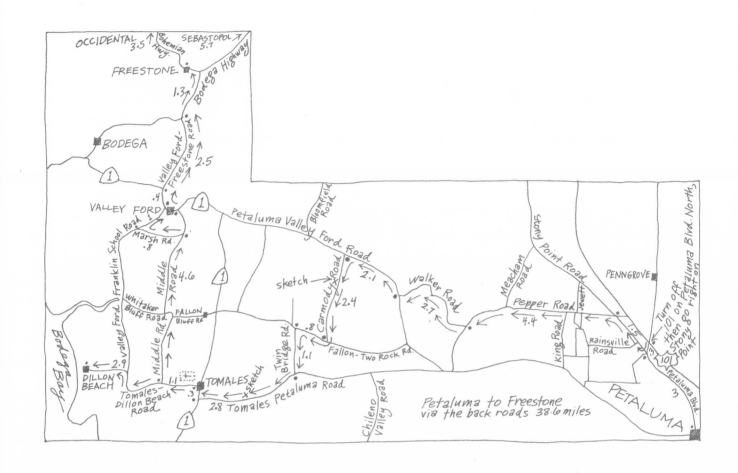

Back roads bring me to Freestone. The town derived its name from a kind of easily worked, or free, sandstone quarry nearby.

I sketch the old, restored hilltop schoolhouse. The original railroad hostelry, known as Hinds Hotel in 1893, is still there, today called Freestone House. I also investigate the interesting plant nursery and zoo.

Old schoolhouse at Freestone, Sonoma County

Coleman Valley Road to the sea

I begin a journey to the coast on Coleman Valley Road off Occidental town's Third Street. The road winds through hilly meadow and forest. Trees are less in evidence as I approach the coast and sheep roam the smooth green hillsides. The road becomes a ridge route with views all around. Fields of low-growing purple iris are in bloom in the spring landscape. Deep green ravines and rows of coastal mountains carry the eye further and further until the sea comes into view. On the ridge above the ocean I sketch the old Irish Hill Ranch, originally owned by the Fitzgeralds. I hear that the ranch owners switched from cows to sheep farming during the Second World War because the lights required for early milkings were banned by wartime coastal blackout controls. It was easier to raise sheep than to lightproof a big, old barn or milk a whole herd of cows in the dark.

From Irish Hill to the sea

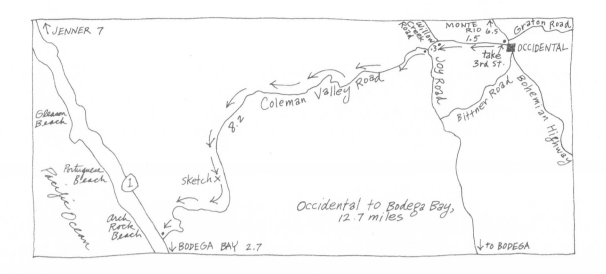

JENNER 7

Coleman Valley Road

8.2

Gleason Beach

Portuguese Beach

1

Pacific Ocean

sketch X

Arch Rock Beach

↓ BODEGA BAY 2.7

MONTE RIO 6.5 1.5

Willow Creek Road

Graton Road

.3

take 3rd St.

OCCIDENTAL

Joy Road

Bittner Road

Bohemian Highway

Occidental to Bodega Bay, 12.7 miles

↓ to BODEGA

20

Willow Creek Road to Jenner

From the end of Occidental's hilly Third
Street, I sketch the historic Union Hotel, where in
the late 1800s dances attracted revelers from
Bodega, Freestone, Valley Ford, Sebastopol, and
even Santa Rosa. The highest railroad bridge west
of the Mississippi was located near here at the time.
It was said of the early town, "It lies in the heart
of a redwood forest, and the old stumps still stand
in the streets." Evidence of early Italian
settlement is still apparent with the flourishing
of Neapolitan restaurants in town.
Also pictured in my drawing is the 1903
Church of St. Philip.

Occidental, Sonoma County

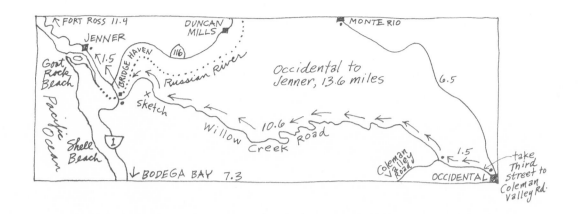

Within the map image:
FORT ROSS 11.4
DUNCAN MILLS
MONTE RIO
JENNER
116
1.5
Goat Rock Beach
BRIDGE HAVEN
Russian River
Occidental to Jenner, 13.6 miles
6.5
Pacific Ocean
sketch
Willow Creek Road
10.6
Shell Beach
1
Coleman Valley Road
1.5
take Third Street to Coleman Valley Rd.
OCCIDENTAL
BODEGA BAY 7.3

I drive the partly unpaved route to Jenner along
Willow Creek Road. It is winding and heavily forested
at times. Cattle chew their cuds and swat
flies with their tails as they lounge among
big ferns in the shade of a redwood grove.
A hawk and a raven swoop and clash with each
other in the sky above.
    I draw a farmhouse nestled in a valley
near the coast where Willow Creek
flows into the Russian River.

Willow Creek farm, Sonoma County

23

Sweetwater landscape, Sonoma County

Roundabout to Armstrong State Park

Westside Road gives views of lush farm country and the thick green of grapevines growing in the summer sun. At Sweetwater Springs turnoff, I sketch a view of a triple-stack hop kiln with Mt. St. Helena in the distance.

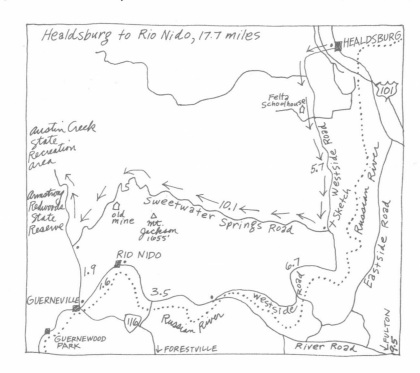

Healdsburg to Rio Nido, 17.7 miles

HEALDSBURG

101

Felta Schoolhouse

austin Creek State Recreation area

5.7

Westside Road

Russian River

Sweetwater Springs Road

10.1

armstrong Redwoods State Reserve

old mine

Mt. Jackson 1655'

x Sketch

Eastside Road

RIO NIDO

6.7

1.9

1.6

3.5

Westside Road

GUERNEVILLE

116

Russian River

↓ FULTON 9.5

GUERNEWOOD PARK

↓ FORESTVILLE

River Road

Hops, used as flavoring for beer, were a major crop in this area at one time. The long vines were hung to dry in these decorative buildings. The hop kilns are now used for a winery.

Sweetwater Springs Road has a primitive feel to it. Skirting Mount Jackson, it undoubtedly was made with a great deal of effort by early road builders. It twists and turns and is a bit steep and narrow — a more adventurous trip than merely continuing around the mountain on Westside Road. For those wishing an effortless, yet scenic route to Armstrong State Park, stay on Westside.

At Armstrong, ancient live redwoods may be viewed.

Back road to Fort Ross

From the wooded hamlet of Cazadero, Fort Ross Road winds up and over the coastal mountains. A fire had charred the landscape a few years back; however, the slow regeneration of the forest is now in process. Burned redwoods are striking new branches and seedling firs are sprouting new spring needles. Closer to the sea, purple iris blooms in quantity. At Fort Ross, a brisk, cool breeze blows across the bluffs where I choose to sketch.

Fort Ross, Sonoma County

Fine restoration has been done on the old Russian fort.
In 1834 the Chief Ruler of the Russian Colonies in America
had described it like this: "There have been erected two
towers with cannons defending all sides of this so-called
fort, which appears to the eyes of the Indians and
local Spaniards, however, as being very strong and
possibly even unconquerable. Within the enclosure...
stand.... the home of the director..., barracks, stores,
and a chapel, kept in cleanliness and order... outside the
fort... are located two company cattle barns, spacious and
distinctively clean, with pens, a small building for
storing milk and making butter, a shed for the Indians, a
threshing floor, and two rows of small company and private
homes with gardens and orchards.... In a clearing... stands a
windmill... at a wharf for canoes are a broad shed and
trading station, a blacksmithery, a tannery, and a bath house."

Back road sign,
Napa County

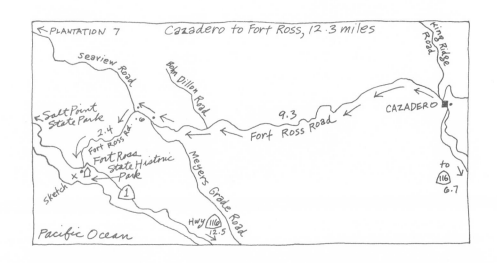

Within the map (img_1):
PLANTATION 7
Seaview Road
Bohn Dillon Road
King Ridge Road
CAZADERO
9.3
Fort Ross Road
Salt Point State Park
2.4
Fort Ross Rd.
Fort Ross State Historic Park
Meyers Grade Road
to 116 6.7
Sketch
1
Pacific Ocean
Hwy 116 12.5

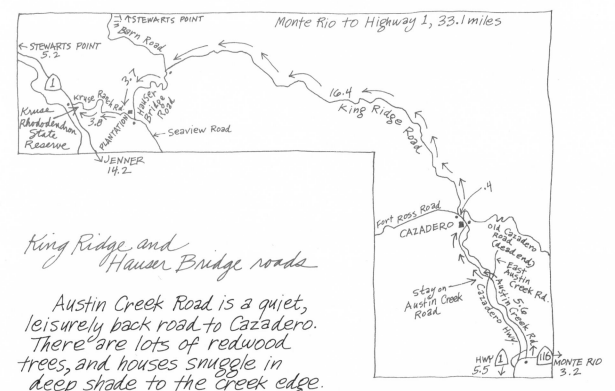

Within the map (img_2):
STEWARTS POINT
Barn Road
STEWARTS POINT 5.2
1
Kruse Ranch Rd.
3.1
Hauser Bridge Road
16.4
King Ridge Road
Kruse Rhododendron State Reserve
3.8
PLANTATION
Seaview Road
JENNER 14.2
Fort Ross Road
CAZADERO
.4
Old Cazadero Road (dead end)
East Austin Creek Rd.
stay on Austin Creek Road
Austin Creek Rd.
Cazadero Hwy.
HWY 1 5.5
116 MONTE RIO 3.2

King Ridge and Hauser Bridge roads

Austin Creek Road is a quiet, leisurely back road to Cazadero. There are lots of redwood trees, and houses snuggle in deep shade to the creek edge. Along King Ridge Road out of Cazadero, long views of the coastal mountain chain are outlined. It is grazing land and the road winds like an old cattle trail, skirting ancient wooden fencing and traversing the crests of dun-colored mountaintops. Hauser Bridge Road then dips down to where a narrow steel bridge crosses the picturesque Gualala River, then up and over another ridge and down to Plantation.

Plantation had a post office and a hotel in earlier days; it is now a private children's camp. As I sketch the Plantation barn, several cars emerge from Kruse Rhododendron State Reserve, their occupants stopping to ask, "Where am I" and "Where are the rhododendrons?"

The rhododendron's rose-tinted blooms appear between March and June. (This was a hot July day.) I proceed through the Reserve after leaving Plantation and note great clumps of rhododendrons disguised as green leaves at this time of year. The red- woods had been logged in the 1890s, and in the 1000-year cycle it takes to return to a redwood forest, the tanbark oak and rhododendron stage has been reached. Some tanbarks have been removed to keep from smothering out the colorful rhododendrons.

The white barn, Plantation, Sonoma County

The store at Stewarts Point, Sonoma County

Stewarts Point to Healdsburg, 49.4 miles

Fish Hatchery and Visitor Center

Warm Springs Dam

Stewarts Point Overlook

ANNAPOLIS

Annapolis Road

SEA RANCH

Indian Rancheria

·x sketch

6.5

STEWARTS POINT

old Steel bridges

Stewarts Point-Skaggs Springs Road   27.5

note: the site of Skaggs Springs is no longer in evidence

Dutcher Creek Rd.

GEYSERVILLE

128

5.2

Canyon Road turn right on Yoakim Bridge Rd.

101

West Dry Creek Road 9.3

Lambert Bridge Road

Dry Creek Rd.

HEALDSBURG

Tin Barn Road

Pacific Ocean

1

FORT ROSS

Westside Road

The Stewarts Point - Skaggs Springs Road

Opposite the quaint 1868 Stewarts Point store, the Stewarts Point-Skaggs Springs Road ascends through dense fir and redwood forest. An old steel bridge spans the Gualala River. I remember hoping that it wouldn't soon be replaced with the usual uninteresting modern concrete crossing. There is access to the river here and a possible picnicking spot.

I view ranges of coastal mountains as the road winds up and over various summits. Skaggs Springs was at one time a celebrated watering place which, in the 1860s, could accommodate 300 people. A writer of the time gave this description of the Springs: "There are here a few acres of tolerable, level fertile land; the rest of the country is pretty slanting; in fact up edgeways, and they pasture goats on both sides of it. There are plenty of deer in the vicinity, but it is very dangerous hunting them; if you should kill one it would be liable to fall on your head."

The road eventually becomes wider and faster as I approach the Warm Springs Dam area. The Stewarts Point Overlook affords a dramatic view of the dam. I take West Dry Creek Road down a narrow valley planted with grapevines and plum trees to Highway 101 and Healdsburg.

33

*Back roads
in apple country*

Apple orchards pattern
the up-and-down
hills west of Sebastopol,
although new housing
and new vineyards have
downed a number of
trees in this picturesque
countryside.

*apples near
Sebastopol,
Sonoma County*

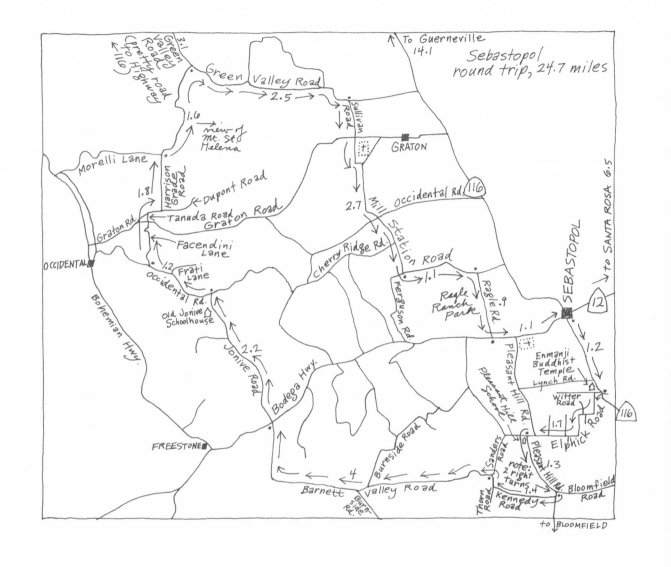

The main town, Sebastopol, was named for the Crimean port in the USSR. In the late 1800s it was famous as the birthplace of canned applesauce. An architectural tour of Sebastopol has been published by the Western Sonoma Historical Society, P.O. Box 816, Sebastopol. It includes a temple, which had traveled in toto from Japan to the Chicago World's Fair (1933-34) and then home to Sebastopol.

The rolling hills and winding roads take me through a varied landscape — from apple-growing areas to deep valleys and meadows. Apple trees give way to oaks and eucalyptus. Along Jonive Road are firs and redwoods and on Harrison Grade I drive past juniper and manzanita before returning to apple country and Sebastopol.

Back roads to the Napa Valley

In the deep shade of its garden I sketch Lachryma Montis (Tears of the Mountain), once the home of General Mariano Guadalupe Vallejo. It was named for the spring that supplied water to both the farm and the early town of Sonoma. In town I stop at the Sonoma League for Historic Preservation, 129 East Spain, to pick up its good walking guide to the town.

I travel the back roads from here into Napa County's Carneros district. Here, near the upper reaches of San Francisco Bay, the climate is cooler. It is a good place to plant wine grapes of the early maturing variety.

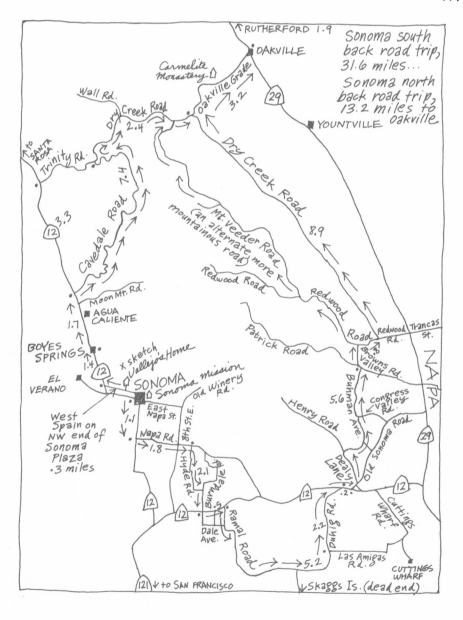

RUTHERFORD 1.9
OAKVILLE
Carmelite Monastery
Wall Rd.
Dry Creek Road 2.4
Oakville Grade 3.2
29
Sonoma south back road trip, 31.6 miles...
Sonoma north back road trip, 13.2 miles to Oakville
YOUNTVILLE
to SANTA ROSA
Trinity Rd.
Cavedale Road 7.4
12 3.3
Dry Creek Road 8.9
Mt. Veeder Road (an alternate more mountainous road)
Redwood Road
Redwood Road
Moon Mt. Rd.
AGUA CALIENTE 1.7
BOYES SPRINGS 1.4
12
EL VERANO
x sketch Vallejo's Home
SONOMA
Sonoma mission
old Winery Rd.
West Spain on NW end of Sonoma Plaza .3 miles
East Napa St. 1.1
15 & 116
Napa Rd. 1.8
Hyde Rd.
Burndale Rd. 2.1
12
12
.5
Dale Ave.
Ramal Road 5.2
121 to SAN FRANCISCO
Patrick Road
Henry Road
Buhman Ave.
Browns Valley 5.6
Congress Valley Rd.
Old Sonoma Road
Redwood Rd.
Trancas St.
NAPA
29
Deay's Lane
12
.2
Duhig Rd. 2.2
Cuttings Wharf Rd.
12
Las Amigas Rd. .8
CUTTINGS WHARF
Skaggs Is. (dead end)

North of Sonoma, I look for Cavedale Road. It winds up into the Mayacamas Range with good views of Sonoma Valley. Toyon, maple, madrone, oak, bay, and fir trees seem to close in over the road. Joining Trinity Road, I travel over the mountains toward Oakville, stopping to enjoy an expansive view of Napa Valley.

Lachryma Montis, Sonoma County

Back road to Middletown

I pass Mark West Springs, where mineral hot springs were discovered in 1857. It had become a popular spa in the 19th century, famous for its sulphur baths. Ancient grapevines twine over the road at this point.

Franz Valley Road winds over the crest of the Mayacamas Range and drops into Franz Valley with a distant view of Mount St. Helena.

I reach Knights Valley, named for Thomas Knight who came to California in 1845. Ida Clayton Road, circling the western side of the mountain, brings me to the view I sketch. It was a mining road in the 1860s and Tom Knight originally came here to work in the mines. Later he became a farmer and lived in a two-story adobe built by José de los Santos Berryessa.

The most famous mine was Great Western Mine where cinnabar was extracted from the earth to produce mercury.

Massive and majestic, Mt. St. Helena, at 4343 feet, rises almost twice as high as surrounding mountains. It was named by Helena de Gagarin, wife of the Governor-General of the Russian colonies in America. On June 20, 1841, she had headed an expedition that ascended the mountain. At the top she christened it St. Helena in honor of the patron saint of the Empress of Russia.

Mt. St. Helena,
Sonoma County

39

Back road to Middletown

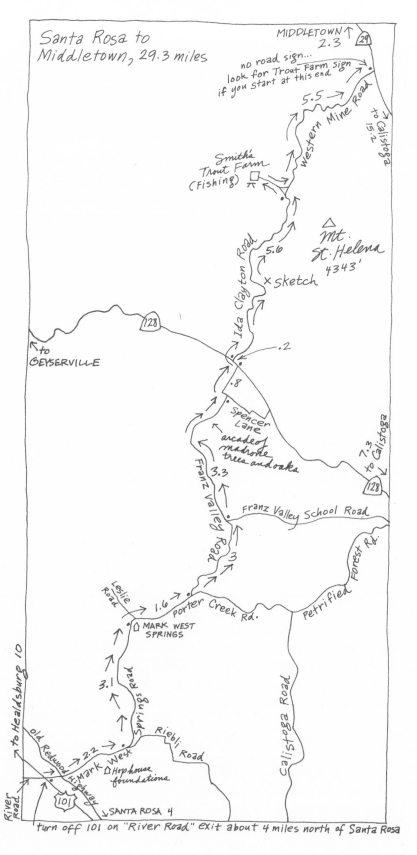

Santa Rosa to
Middletown, 29.3 miles

MIDDLETOWN↑ 29
2.3

no road sign...
look for Trout Farm sign
if you start at this end

5.5 →

Western Mine Road

to Calistoga
15.2

Smith's
Trout Farm
(Fishing)

Mt.
St. Helena
4343'

5.6

✕ sketch

Ida Clayton Road

.2

to
GEYSERVILLE

128

.8

Spencer
Lane

arcade of
madrone
trees and oaks

7.3
to Calistoga

128

3.3

Franz Valley Road

Franz Valley School Road

3

Petrified Forest Rd.

Leslie
Road

1.6 →

Porter Creek Rd.

MARK WEST
SPRINGS

Calistoga Road

3.1

Springs Road

Riebli
Road

to Healdsburg 10

old Redwood Highway

2.2 →

Mark West

Hop house
foundations

River Road

101

SANTA ROSA 4

turn off 101 on "River Road" exit about 4 miles north of Santa Rosa

40

Lower Lake back road and the road to Knoxville

↑to WILLIAMS

WILLIAMS 12

5

Cortina School Road

• Hillgate Road

↑to CLEARLAKE OAKS

20

16

Green Road (unmarked)

14.7 →→

ARBUCKLE

→ 5 →

to WOODLAND

53

Lower Lake to Arbuckle, 51.1 miles

Lower Lake to St. Helena, 59.6 miles

starting from this end look for sign for Road 40 (Rayhouse Road)

Sand Creek

(Road 41)

"Y" in road keep to right

LOWER LAKE

Cache Creek Canyon Regional Park

→ 5.1

5

• Road 41A

11.4

• Reiff Road

x sketch

Rayhouse Rd.

29

no road sign

Reiff Road →

14.9 →

(rough road) (not open in winter)

8.1

x sketch

KNOXVILLE (site)

16

x sketch of mailbox

MIDDLETOWN

Butts Canyon Road

18.2

to → WOODLAND

↑to GEYSERVILLE

Pope Valley Road

Pope Valley Cross Road

Pope Canyon Road

8.4 →

Lake Berryessa

29

follow sign to "St. Helena"

128

POPE VALLEY

.6

Chiles and Pope Valley Road

CALISTOGA

29 7.2

ANGWIN

Napa Valley

5.5

Deer Park Howell Mt. Rd.

.5

to St. Helena
1.5 ↓

Back road from Lower Lake

Lower Lake has a colorful mining town look to it. The 1868
IOOF building and the old jail still stand, as does the bulky
brick 1877 schoolhouse with its second-story dance hall.
    Morgan Valley Road heads east from here through farm
country and into steeper hills where blue-green oaks
and black-barked serpentine pines predominate.
    Unmarked, Reiff Road goes east into Yolo County through
the Blue Ridge Mountains to Highway 16 and Cache Creek
Regional Park.   I stop at the Reiff Ranch to sketch
a barn built by the family in 1930. Mr. Reiff talks of
fixing the structure because the mudsills, which had
been its foundation, are gone and barn supports have
gone askew.   We agree that all a well-built barn needs
is good roofing and a proper foundation and it will
last forever.   The road from here to Highway 16
bumps and joggles. It is a slow-going back road
(and "closed during winter," a sign reports).   I pass old,
rusty mining buildings and, at another point, enjoy
dramatic views of rugged mountains.   Road 41 (Sand
Creek Road) affords scenic views of the fertile
valley far below. And, on topping the ridge, a view of
mountains and hills, superimposed one on the
next, extends as far as the eye can see.

42

Reiff Barn,
Lake County

44

The road to Knoxville (map, page 41)

In July grassy slopes shimmer with soft, golden light. Groves of oak trees make blue-green silhouettes on the hillsides and canyons.

At Knoxville I sketch the ghostly Manhattan Quicksilver Mine Headquarters building. Several 14-inch, spotted, black and tan alligator lizards eye me at close range and I shoo off the fierce-looking creatures with my drawing pad. Unusually curious, they return again and again, enjoying my little game.

South of Knoxville, Lake Berryessa gleams bright blue contrasting with the surrounding dun-colored hills.

Manhattan Quicksilver Mine Office, Knoxville, Napa County

46

Round Valley Church, Covelo, Mendocino County

Back road through Mendocino National Forest

This forest was conserved for the nation by President Theodore Roosevelt in 1907. Highway 162 from Williams continues just a few miles north of Elk Creek, climbing high into brush-covered mountains. I stopped to look at Grindstone Canyon and read a forest service sign pointing out brush clearance projects. Grass is planted for the deer and cow populations, instead of allowing brush to proliferate.

Up higher I am in a vast conifer forest with views of adjoining mountain ranges. As I proceed further the land opens up with more grazing areas. Views are often magnificent.

I reach Covelo in Round Valley and draw the Methodist Church. A squirrel looks out of the faded pink and white bell tower while woodpeckers fly back and forth adding new acorn holes to it. A poster in the church entrance announces that in a few days the church will host a free movie, "The Horror of Dracula."

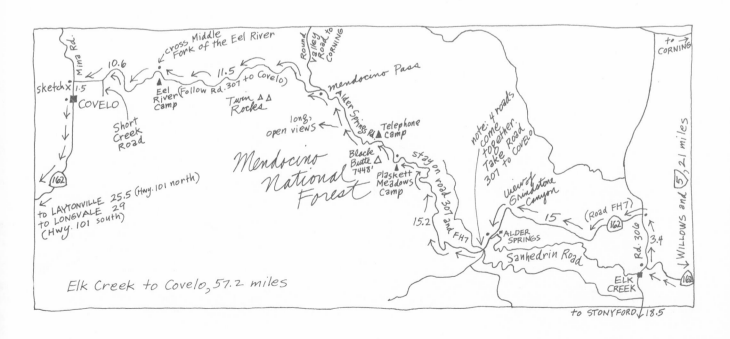

cross Middle Fork of the Eel River
to CORNING
Mina Rd.
10.6
11.5
Round Valley Road to CORNING
Mendocino Pass
sketch X 1.5
COVELO
Eel River Camp
(Follow Rd. 307 to Covelo)
Twin Rocks
Alder Springs Rd.
Telephone Camp
note: 4 roads come together. Take Road 307 to COVELO
to WILLOWS and 5, 21 miles
Short Creek Road
long, open views
Mendocino National Forest
Black Butte 7448'
Plaskett Meadows Camp
stay on road 307
View of Grindstone Canyon
to LAYTONVILLE 25.5 (Hwy. 101 north)
to LONGVALE 29 (Hwy. 101 south)
162
15.2
road 307 and FH7
ALDER SPRINGS
15
(Road FH7)
162
Rd. 306
3.4
Sanhedrin Road
ELK CREEK
162

Elk Creek to Covelo, 57.2 miles

to STONYFORD 18.5

The road to Blocksburg

North of Garberville, in the Avenue of the Giants, I draw an almost 8-foot-wide redwood stump. Over the years countless initials have been carved in the wood. One carving is somewhat more profound than the others. It states "Thou art God."

Leaving the great redwoods, I travel inland through hilly forest and meadow. Big views of mountain scenery appear, sometimes on both sides of the road as I drive higher. They are awe-inspiring. I bypass Fort Seward, a military post in 1861.

Redwoods, Humboldt County

At Blocksburg I get permission to sketch the town's oldest barn and march across a field of thistles and manure piles to sit in the shade of an old fruit tree. At the time the barn was built the town had seven bars and two barbershops. It was a tanbark-collecting center from which the bark was hauled to a faraway tannery in Willits. Sheep raising was big also and there was some manganese ore mining. The old Mail Ridge Stage Route north from San Francisco passed through here when Mr. Blocksburgher, the town's namesake, had been a storekeeper and wool merchant.

From Bridgeville — also a stop on the old Mail Ridge Stage Route — I climb up a long, steep gravel road. The climb is worth it for I am now richly rewarded with vast mountain views. Metal barn roofs glisten in the distance. I pass the charming community of Freshwater on my journey to Eureka.

Blocksburg barn,
Humboldt County

50

51

The road to Blocksburg

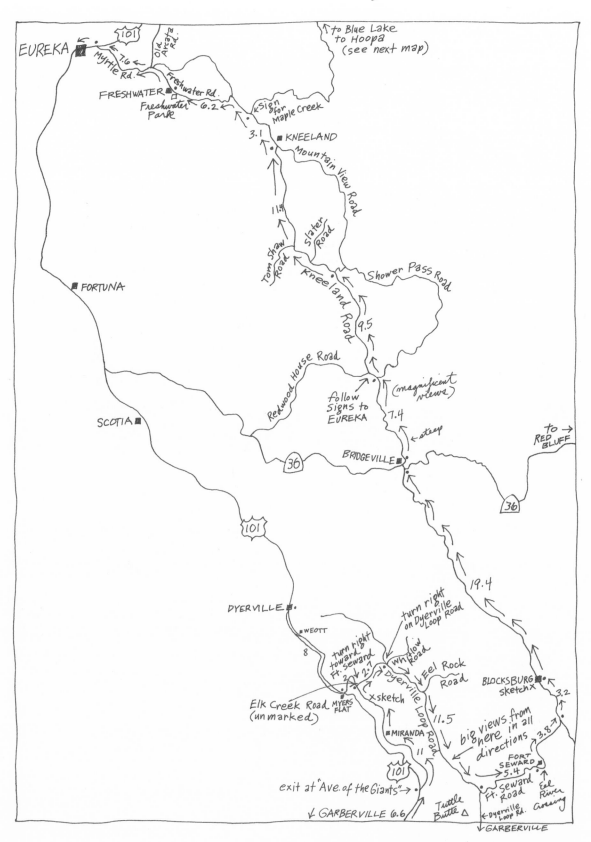

to Blue Lake
to Hoopa
(see next map)

EUREKA

101

Myrtle Rd. 7.6 ←

Old Arcata Rd.

FRESHWATER

Freshwater Rd. 6.2 ←

Freshwater Park

Sign for Maple Creek

3.1

KNEELAND

Mountain View Road

11.4

Tom Shaw Road

Slater Road

Kneeland Road

Shower Pass Road

9.5

Redwood House Road

follow signs to EUREKA

(magnificent views)

7.4

← steep

FORTUNA

SCOTIA

36

BRIDGEVILLE

to RED BLUFF →

36

101

19.4

DYERVILLE

WEOTT

8

turn right toward Ft. Seward

2 2.1

turn right on Dyerville Loop Road

Whitlow Road

Eel Rock Road

BLOCKSBURG sketch X

3.2

Elk Creek Road (unmarked)

MYERS FLAT

X sketch

Dyerville Loop Road

11.5

big views from here in all directions

MIRANDA

3.8

11

FORT SEWARD 5.4

101

exit at "Ave. of the Giants" →

Ft. Seward Road

Eel River Crossing

↓ GARBERVILLE 6.6

Tuttle Butte △

← Dyerville Loop Rd.

↓ GARBERVILLE

The road to Hoopa Valley and to Lady Bird Johnson Grove

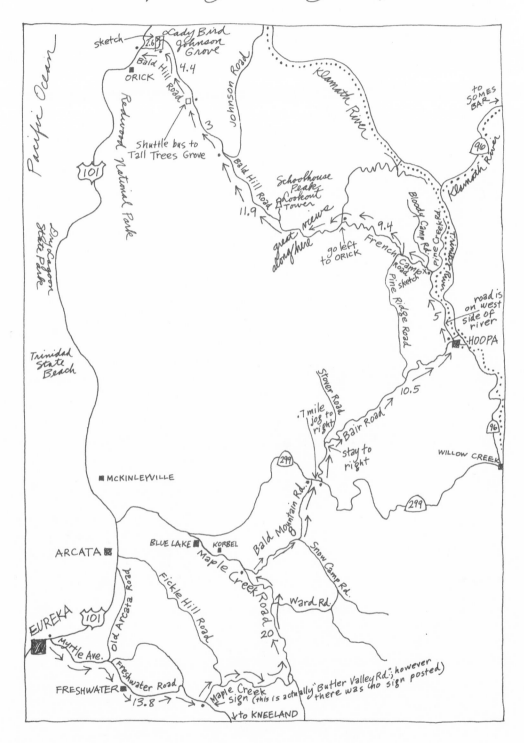

Pacific Ocean

sketch

Del Norge State Park

Redwood National Park

Lady Bird Johnson Grove

2.6

Bald Hill Road

4.4

ORICK

Johnson Road

3

Shuttle bus to Tall Trees Grove

101

Bald Hill Road

11.9

Schoolhouse Peak Lookout Tower

great views along here

go left to ORICK

Klamath River

to SOMES BAR →

96

French road sketch

Camp

Pine Ridge Road

9.4

Bloody Camp Rd.

Trinity River

Tish Tang Creek

Klamath River

road is on west side of river

5

HOOPA

Trinidad State Beach

Stover Road

.7 mile jog to right

Bair Road

10.5

stay to right

299

96

WILLOW CREEK

McKINLEYVILLE

299

Bald Mountain Rd.

ARCATA

BLUE LAKE   KORBEL

Maple Creek Road

Snow Camp Rd.

Ward Rd.

EUREKA

101

Old Arcata Road

Fickle Hill Road

20

Myrtle Ave.

Freshwater Road

FRESHWATER

13.8

Maple Creek sign (this is actually "Butter Valley Rd."; however there was no sign posted)

↓ to KNEELAND

Hoopa Valley, Humboldt County   55

The road to Hoopa Valley — (map, page 53)

Butler Valley Road east of Eureka meanders
north. A winding mountain road then proceeds
across the Mad River and picturesque Maple Creek.
Near Lord Ellis Summit, forest foliage joins overhead
to become a tunnel of green. Firs, cedars, tanbark,
oak, and madrone line Bair Road to Hoopa Valley.
Leaving Hoopa, I sketch a view with the Klamath River
glinting in the sun, winding its way through the green
valley, fine mountain scenery all around. A madrone
tree offers shade and drops stiff, dry leaves about
me with each slight breeze.

Hoopa Valley to Lady Bird Johnson Grove (map, page 53)

The long pull uphill from Hoopa Valley finally
emerges on top of the world (or so it seems!). The views
exhilarate and lift the spirit. I travel through high
pastureland and descend near the coast to
Lady Bird Johnson Grove. There I draw a
so-called Goose Pen Tree (redwood), which pioneers
had, on occasion, used to confine small livestock
and fowl. Oxalis, sword fern, salal, and evergreen
huckleberry grow at its redwood base. Scarred
by ancient fires, the tree itself remains alive and well,
a giant in this truly magnificent stand of redwoods.
Experiencing this place is enriching and inspiring.

Goose Pen redwood, Humboldt County

57

The Salmon Alps, Siskiyou County

Back road along the Salmon River to Scott Valley

From Somes Bar and Highway 96 and from Forks of
Salmon to Cecilville, a narrow, paved, winding, sometimes
one-way road clings to the rocky ledge high above
the roaring Salmon River. A sign early on had
warned motorists that slow travel and honking of
the horn on blind curves might be necessary.
    Views of the Salmon Alps appear as I approach
Cecilville. From Cecilville the road becomes straighter
and smoother (and thereby less interesting). At the
Salmon Summit and the Pacific Crest Trailhead heliport
I sketch 7,790-foot Eagle Peak and include Billy's
Peak and Battle Mountain. They are all lined up in
splendid array from this scenic viewpoint.
    I descend from here to Callahan at the foot of Scott Valley.

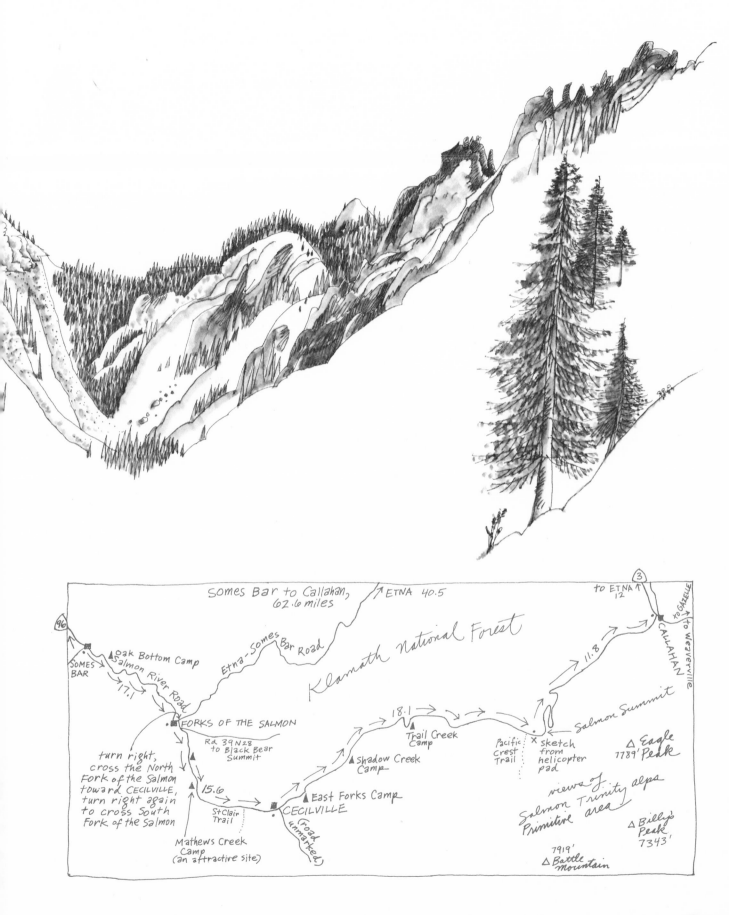

Somes Bar to Callahan, 62.6 miles

ETNA 40.5

to ETNA 12

(3)

to GAZELLE
to WEAVERVILLE

(96)

Klamath National Forest

Oak Bottom Camp

SOMES BAR

Etna-Somes Bar Road

Salmon River Road

17.1

CALLAHAN

11.8

FORKS OF THE SALMON

Rd 39N28 to Black Bear Summit

18.1

Trail Creek Camp

Salmon Summit

turn right, cross the North Fork of the Salmon toward CECILVILLE, turn right again to cross South Fork of the Salmon

15.6

Shadow Creek Camp

Pacific Crest Trail

sketch from helicopter pad

△ Eagle 7789' Peak

StClair Trail

East Forks Camp

CECILVILLE (road unmarked)

views of Salmon Trinity alps Primitive area

Mathews Creek Camp (an attractive site)

7919' △ Battle Mountain

△ Billy's Peak 7343'

59

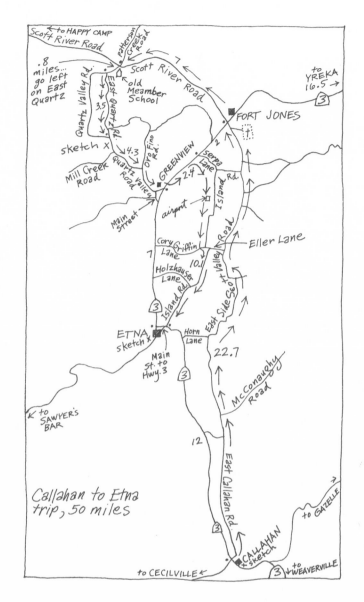

to HAPPY CAMP
Scott River Road
Patterson Creek Road
.8 miles... go left on East Quartz
Scott River Road
old Meamber School
to YREKA 16.5 →
3
East Quartz Rd.
Quartz Valley Rd.
3.5
sketch x
4.3
Mill Creek Road
Oro Fino Rd.
Quartz Valley Road
GREENVIEW
2.4
serpa Lane
FORT JONES
Island Rd.
Main Street
airport
Island Rd.
Cory Griffin Lane
Eller Lane
7
10.1
Holzhauser Lane
East Side Scott Valley Road
Island Rd.
3
ETNA sketch x
Horn Lane
Main St. to Hwy. 3
3
22.7
McConaughy Road
x to SAWYER'S BAR
12
Callahan to Etna trip, 50 miles
East Callahan Rd.
to GAZELLE
CALLAHAN x sketch
3
to CECILVILLE ←
3 ↓ to WEAVERVILLE

a trip through
Scott Valley

The valley was named for John Scott, who had led a group of miners into the area in 1850. He discovered gold, and Scott Valley became a rich mining region. Today the valley is green with agricultural crops. Sprinklers sprinkle and black angus cows browse in the field.

In Quartz Valley, where gold camps once flourished, I sketch a neat, white schoolhouse and its monumental stone marker.

At Etna, originally known as Rough and Ready Mills, I draw the library building with its massive flagpole. As you approach the town, you can see the pole towering over all the other structures. I asked at the post office, city hall, and finally, a corner delicatessan to find out the height of the pole. The gentleman who told me it was 136½ feet (two feet shorter than the one at neighboring Fort Jones) wondered whether I wanted to climb it. I said no, but I'd enjoy seeing someone else do it!

White Schoolhouse , Siskiyou County

Etna's flagpole,
Siskiyou County

ETNA FREE LIBRARY and READING ROOM

POST OFFICE
CALLAHAN * CAL. 26014

Sign at Callahan, Siskiyou County

Back road from Scott Valley

The Farrington Blacksmith Shop, the General Store, and the Ranch Hotel still stand at Callahan. I draw the old sign over the post office entrance next to the General Store and chat with the owner whose great-grandfather had built these historic edifices. In the 1860s this locality was a stage stop along the principal wagon road north to Oregon.

The road going east from Callahan rises gently to almost 5,000 feet through pine and cedar forest, then suddenly drops toward Interstate 5 near Gazelle.

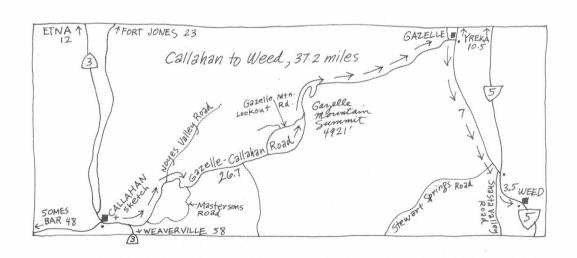

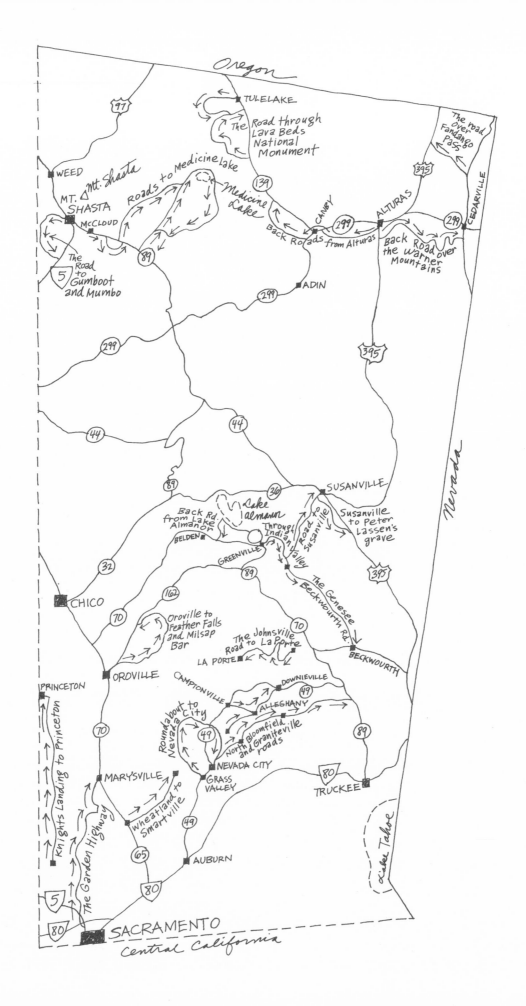

Oregon

97

TULELAKE

The Road through
Lava Beds
National
Monument

The road
over
Fandango
Pass

WEED   Mt. Shasta

MT.
SHASTA

Roads to Medicine Lake

Medicine
Lake

139

395

CEDARVILLE

McCLOUD

89

CANBY   ALTURAS   299

299

Back Roads from Alturas   Back Road over
the Warner
Mountains

5   The
Road
to
Gumboot
and Mumbo

299   ADIN

299

395

44   44

395

Nevada

89   36   SUSANVILLE

Lake
Almann

Back Rd.
from Lake
Almanor

Susanville
to Peter
Lassen's
grave

32   BELDEN

Through
Indian
Valley

Road to Susanville

GREENVILLE   89

395

The Genesee
Beckwourth Rd.

162

CHICO

70   Oroville to
Feather Falls
and Milsap
Bar

70

The Johnsville
Road to La Porte

BECKWOURTH

LA PORTE

89

PRINCETON   OROVILLE   CAMPTONVILLE   DOWNIEVILLE

Roundabout to
Nevada City   49   ALLEGHANY

49   80

North Bloomfield
and Graniteville
roads

89

70   NEVADA CITY

MARYSVILLE   GRASS
VALLEY   TRUCKEE

Wheatland to
Smartville   49   Lake Tahoe

65   AUBURN

5

80   80

SACRAMENTO

Central California

Knights Landing to Princeton

The Garden Highway

Northeastern California

It is heartening to think that however loud the
main arteries of traffic may become, there are
back roads existing in quietude and natural
beauty.   I leave the insistent, fretful
clamor of the freeway and travel the lonely
back roads. Their untainted atmosphere and
the closeness of trees and roadside
flowers are of infinite attraction to me.
It wouldn't be practical to pave or
straighten these roads. They serve
no profitable purpose, and for that
I am thankful.

Monkey flower, Placer County

Castle Crags, Siskiyou County

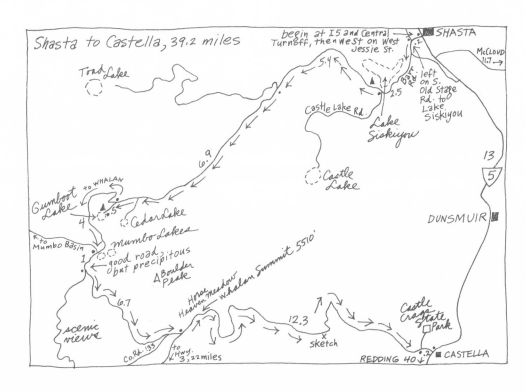

Shasta to Castella, 39.2 miles

begin at I5 and Central Turnoff, then west on West Jessie St. ■ SHASTA

McCLOUD 11.7 →

Toad Lake

5.4

2.5

left on S. Old Stage Rd. to Lake Siskiyou

Castle Lake Rd.

Lake Siskiyou

6.9

13
5

Castle Lake

DUNSMUIR ■

to WHALAN

Gumboot Lake

.5

4

Cedar Lake

to Mumbo Basin

Mumbo Lakes

1

good road but precipitous

Boulder Peak

Horse Heaven meadow   Whalan Summit 5510'

Castle Crags State Park

6.7

scenic views

12.3

Co. Rd. 133

to Hwy. 3, 22 miles

sketch

REDDING 40 ↓ .2 ■ CASTELLA

The road to Gumboot and Mumbo

I pass tranquil Lake Siskiyou and ascend the rugged, rocky canyon. A rushing stream tumbles and splashes downward on my left. Gumboot Lake, cradled in granite in this high mountain wilderness, deeply reflects the blue of the sky. There are views near Mumbo Lake of far distant mountain ranges of northern California, including the high Trinity Alps. Finally I see the impressive Castle Crags and stop to draw its soft gray-colored prominence in the early morning light. It has been a fine trip for the beauty of mountain places, long views, and impressive high country forests.

67

Roads to Medicine Lake

The trip to Medicine Lake begins with stops to view McCloud River Falls. Upper and Lower Falls are easy enough to find; Middle Falls, however, is not marked. The roar can be heard from the roadway, so I follow the sound. There is a sheer cliff to be wary of and therefore this is no place for small children. All three falls are well worth viewing as they churn over rock ledges with a resounding roar. But Middle and Upper Falls are the most dramatic.

There are three routes from the McCloud area to Medicine Lake. Route 13, the road I follow, is dusty but affords closer views of Mount Shasta.

I see Paint Pot Crater, just visible from the road at one point, then Pumice Mountain. On Medicine Lake Road I pass at the very foot of Little Glass Mountain where great black chunks of obsidian glisten in the sunshine.

Back road musician,
Lower Falls, Siskiyou County

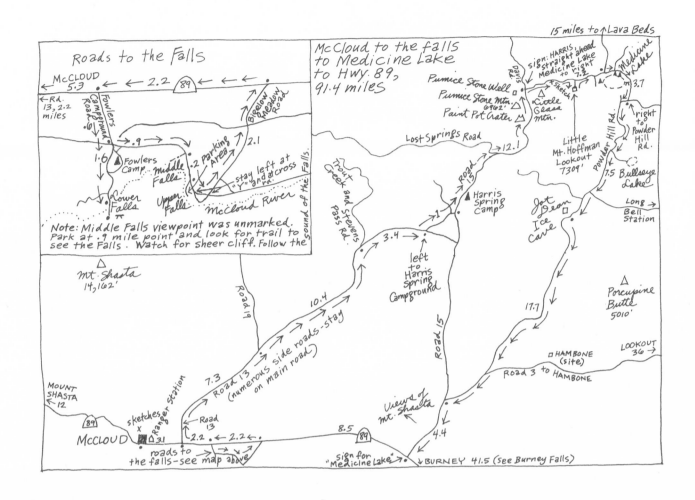

I stop to sketch a particularly dramatic view of Mount Shasta, the helter-skelter profile of Little Glass Mountain in the middle distance. At Little Mount Hoffman lookout a 360-degree view of the world is presented below. The less-than-a-mile drive to the lookout, though precipitous, should be done.

The view of the entire Little Glass Mountain lava flow is particularly interesting from this point.

Medicine Lake proves a lovely, protected, bright blue body of water, and there's a good view of it from the picnic grounds. You have the option of either going further to see Lava Beds National Monument or returning toward McCloud. Jot Dean Ice Cave is on the way to McCloud. It has its own mystic sense of beauty with subtle colorings and dripping sound effects.

Mount Shasta, Siskiyou County

In McCloud I explore
the streets of this
quaint company town.
I travel out East
Columbero, go north
on Shasta and east
on Mill Street.
   Past the big mill
I follow Firenze
Street and North
Street back to the
mill. Following West
Columbero, I take
Hennessy Way to
Tucci, Walnut, and
Oak. I draw the
Bradshaw House,
former lumber
executive residence
near Lawndale Court
off Main, and the
log church. It
   occurs to me that
the chocolate brown
church with its
whipped cream
colored seams
actually looks quite
appetizing.

The Bradshaw House, McCloud,
Siskiyou County

72

St. Joseph's, the chocolate brown church,
McCloud, Siskiyou County

75

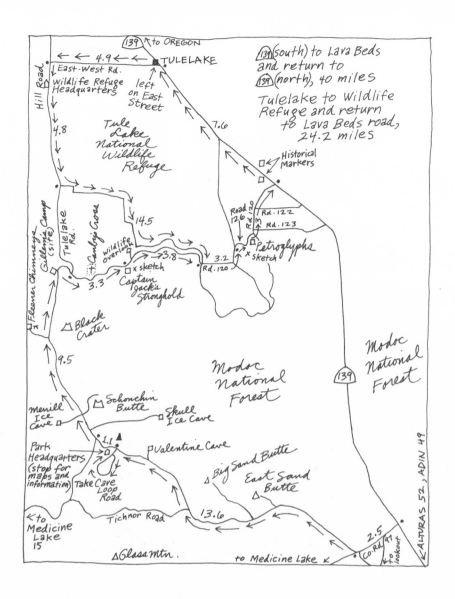

The road through Lava Beds National Monument

There are some 14 or 15 caves to explore near park headquarters. Mushpot Cave is well lit, but flashlights are a necessity for the others. They have colorful names which invite exploration, like Golden Dome, Hopkins Chocolate, and Hercules Leg.

I sketch at Captain Jack's Stronghold, where the Modoc tribe made the U.S. Army pay dearly for victory over the intransigent Indians. As I walk the path through the stronghold I realize how 60 rugged Indians could hold back an army of 600 for five months.

Captain Jack's Stronghold,
Siskiyou and Modoc Counties   77

If it's not too late in the day and you're not in a rush to go on, you could double back to the Tulelake Road (see map) and take the Wildlife Tour Route back to Lava Beds Monument. Otherwise, it might be best to stay overnight in Tulelake and leave the Wildlife Tour for the next day, which is what I decide to do.

At the Petroglyphs I sketch ancient markings, enjoying their simple designs. I watch swallows flying around their mud nests.

On the Wildlife Tour I see ducks of all sorts, herons, white pelicans, Canadian geese, varieties of seabirds, thousands of shiny blue dragonflies, locusts, bees, and a lively assortment of unnamed creatures.

Petroglyphs, Lava Beds National Monument, Modoc County

Back road over the Warner Mountains

I leave Alturas and stop at scenic Dorris Reservoir.
The surface of the reservoir is placid, the morning sun
glinting off the water. A flight of honking geese make
a "V" formation overhead. Grazing horses on a
nearby shore look like cutouts on the horizon.
    The Warner Mountains in the distance, snow still
lingering on Squaw Peak, beckon me. The road
goes through juniper and pine forest, crosses
    several streams, and gently ascends into the Warners.

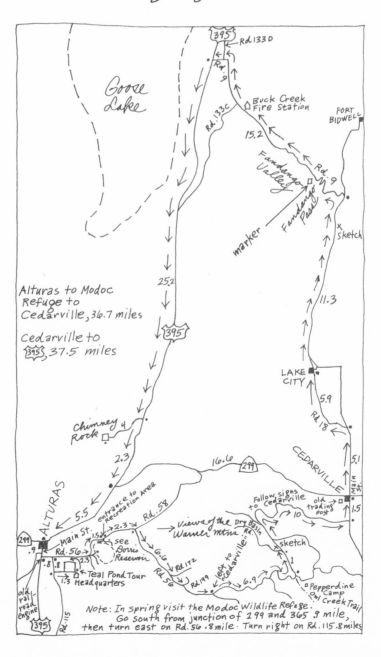

Goose Lake

Rd. 133 D

Rd. 9

Rd. 133 c

Buck Creek Fire Station

FORT BIDWELL

15.2

Fandango Valley

Rd. 9

marker

Fandango Pass

sketch

11.3

25.2

395

Alturas to Modoc
Refuge to
Cedarville, 36.7 miles

Cedarville to
395, 37.5 miles

LAKE CITY

5.9

Rd. 18

Chimney Rock

2.3

16.6

299

CEDARVILLE

5.1

ALTURAS

5.5

entrance to Recreation Area

Rd. 58

Follow signs to Cedarville

old trading post

1.5

Main St.

2.3

Views of the Warner mtns

Dry Basin Rd.

10

299

.9

1.5

see Dorris Reservoir

Rd. 56

2.3

6.6

Rd. 172

Rd. 56

Rd. 199

left to Cedarville

sketch

1

6.9

Teal Pond Tour Headquarters

1.3

Pepperdine Camp

Owl Creek Trail

old railroad engine

395

Rd. 115

Note: In spring visit the Modoc Wildlife Refuge.
Go south from junction of 299 and 365 .9 mile,
then turn east on Rd. 56 .8 mile. Turn right on Rd. 115 .8 miles

At the summit I draw a twisted and all but downed juniper. It expresses well the ferocity of winter storms at this altitude. Grasshoppers make clicking noises, an unseen bird sings, a cool light breeze whooshes through the pines, flies buzz, and range cattle come to stare at me.

From this point the road levels off, then descends toward Cedarville in Surprise Valley. Wagon trains came through here in the 1860s, and James Townsend built a trading post in 1865. He was killed by Indians in 1866. William Cressler and John Bonner bought the Townsend building in 1867 and turned it into a combination trading post and store. What is left of it can still be seen in the town park on Center Street between Highway 299 and Bonner Street.

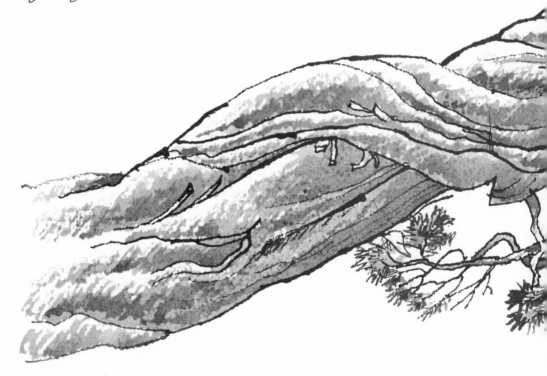

Twisted Juniper,
Warner Mountains, Modoc County

The road over Fandango Pass (see map, page 79)

I travel from Cedarville to the hamlet of Lake City, enjoying sweeping views of Surprise Valley and Upper Lake. Early pioneers were surprised to find a green valley after leaving the barren landscape of Nevada; thereby the name, Surprise Valley. I sketch the inventive antelope and deer horn arrangement at the Hanks Ranch and talk to a charming 88-year-old ranch woman who looks every bit the pioneer in big, floppy hat and one-piece dress. Her gnarled hands point to some cows and calves moving past. She is worried about the whereabouts of a particular calf.

HANKS · RANCH

Back road ranch sign, Modoc County

The approach to Fandango is steep. The Peter
Lassen and Applegate trails come together here, then
part again on the other side of the Warners.
Lassen goes south, Applegate north.   A massacre took
place along this trail sometime between 1846 and 1850.
It is said that Indians attacked while pioneers were
dancing the fandango. The fandangoists were completely
wiped out.   Today I enjoy the sweeping view across
Fandango Valley; cows grazing on the opposite side
look like slowly moving specks.

Back Roads from alturas

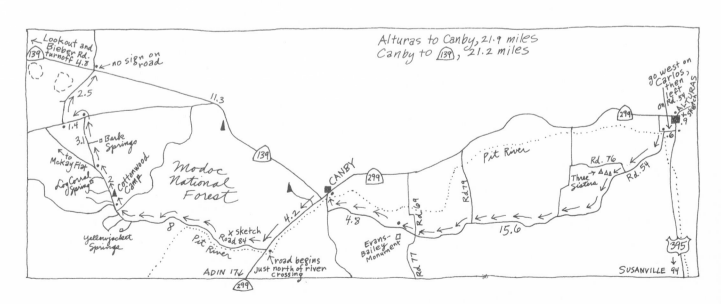

The Court House, Alturas, Modoc County

Back roads of Alturas (map, page 83)

Before leaving Alturas, I admire the solidly elegant bulk of the Modoc County Court House. To sketch it I gain permission to sit on the lawn surrounding the chalk white golden-domed building. 1914 is the date on its facade, and F. J. DeLongchamps was the architect. Niles Hotel is another notable building in Alturas.

When you visit the Chamber of Commerce you are in the original County Recorder Office of Modoc County. To the rear is the old jail.

I travel the Centerville Road west and enjoy broad views of agricultural land and juniper forest. Yellow daisies line the roadway at times, pretty faces turned to the morning sun.

On a hill to the south a white marker commemorates the death of S.D. Evans and Joe Bailey, killed by Indians in July 1861 while driving 900 head of beef cattle to the mines in Virginia City, Nevada.

NAVY ITS NOT JUST A JOB ITS AN ADVENTURE

GO AIR FORCE
USAF REC OFFICE

Going west I reach Canby, named for
the U.S. General of the Modoc War, and
turn left to locate County Road 84 and
the Pit River. I enjoy the scenery along
the lazily flowing stream and pause to
draw one of the views. Cows scratching their
backs on low juniper branches stop to moo.
Only two cowboys in pickup trucks pass
in one and a half hours. The road has
the essence of an old covered wagon trail.

(map, page 83)

The Pit River, Modoc County

Back road from Lake Almanor

The road hugs the shore of Butt Valley Reservoir. It is a pretty body of water despite the eye-jarring power-line structures. I cross the dam spillway and proceed down toward the rushing Feather River. What a colossal canyon! I descend steep slopes with views of forested mountainsides and clouds feathering out along mountain tops. At Caribou, an attractive PG&E Company village, there is a sign, "Fishermen Welcome." I picnic nearby with a view of the Forebay and the impressive cliffs opposite. I continue along the road, stopping to watch a gold-sluicing operation in the river. The road ends at Highway 70 near Belden town and the Eby Stamp Mill roadside rest.

Road block, Plumas County

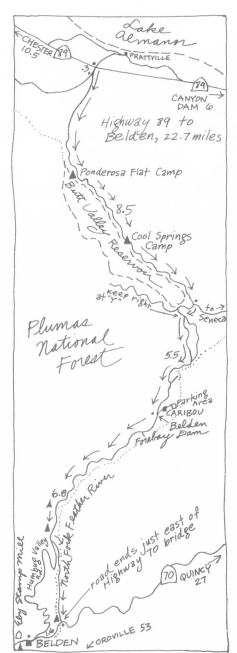

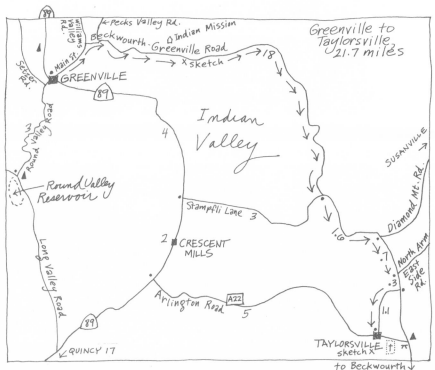

Back road through Indian Valley

I travel from Greenville, long a center of quartz mining activity. It has a distinctive California mining and lumber town look about it. The town is located at one end of broad and beautiful Indian Valley. In winter there are views of surrounding snow-capped peaks. I stop to sketch old Wheelock Shingle Mill with Mount Hough and Grizzly Peak in the background.

The old Wheelock Shingle mill,
Indian Valley, Plumas County

91

At Taylorsville I search the
pioneer cemetery for the monument
marking the grave of the town's namesake, Jobe
Taylor, who settled here in 1852. (I find it.)
This is a village of quaint rural charm with
old houses along shady streets, a white
steepled church, and many barns.

Taylorsville Community Church, 1875

Crescent Mills roundabout to Taylorsville,
or on to Susanville

I sketch a barn full of wood along the way
at a ranch homesteaded by the Peter Hereford family.

Crescent
Mills to
Susanville,
34.8 miles

SUSANVILLE
Gold Run Rd.
to ALTURAS
444
47 89
94
6
94
4.5
4
36
395
Lake Almanor
38
36
Peter Lassen grave
9
395
Rd. to Moonlight V.
Rd. to Fleming Sheep Camp
Rd. to Westwood
15.4
Rd. to Morton Creek
road quality on the primitive side
JANESVILLE
Road to Shake Cabin
Road to Moonlight Valley
Road to Antelope Lake
3 roads come together. take road on left to Susanville
Engle Mine ruins
5.4
CANYON DAM 9
89
GREENVILLE
4 89
Stampfli Lane
CRESCENT MILLS
4.5
sketch×
5
Diamond Mtn. Road
×sketch
6.2
North Arm East Side Rd.
Antelope Lake
Note: This is an alternate drive back to Taylorsville if you elect not to drive the sometimes primitive road to Susanville.
TAYLORSVILLE
QUINCY 23
BECKWOURTH

Hereford Ranch barn, near Taylorsville, Plumas County

The North Arm of Indian Valley is a grand, green expanse bounded by forested mountains.

I draw the valley in the silent, sunny morning. Ants crawl up my legs, bees hum, and the work of woodpeckers echoes across the valley.

You can return to Indian Valley via North Arm East Side Road at the valley's end.

I choose to go over the mountains to Susanville. The road becomes primitive in places; eventually the pine forest thins out, and I descend to the pleasant farming country around Susanville.

The North arm of Indian Valley, Plumas County

97

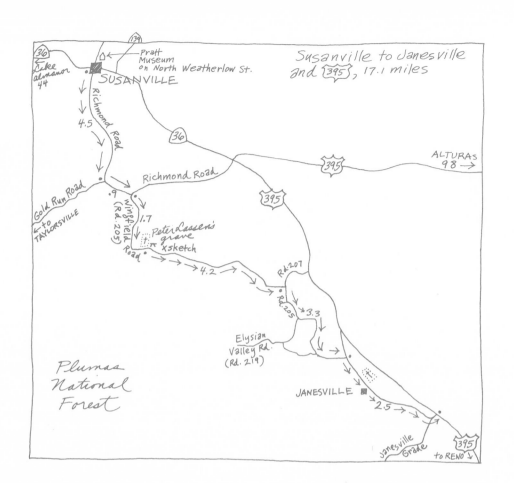

Pratt
Museum
on North Weatherlow St.

Susanville to Janesville
and 395, 17.1 miles

SUSANVILLE

ALTURAS
98 →

Lake
almanor
44

Richmond Road

4.5

Gold Run Road

to TAYLORSVILLE

Richmond Road

395

.9

Wingfield Road (Rd. 205)

1.7

Peter Lassen's
grave
x sketch

4.2

Rd. 207

Rd. 205

3.3

Elysian
Valley Rd.
(Rd. 219)

Plumas
National
Forest

JANESVILLE

2.5

Janesville
Grade

395

to RENO ↓

Isaac Roop was the first white settler in Honey Lake Valley. Susanville, in fact, was named for his first daughter. The Roop log cabin still stands in the city park on Weatherlow Street as does the William Pratt Memorial Museum.

I travel from here to Peter Lassen's grave. Lassen came here from Denmark when he was 29, lived in Indian Valley for awhile and then settled in this area in 1855. Unfortunately, it may not have been a good choice since he was killed here by Indians on April 26, 1859, at age 66.

I sketch a decorative rail fence, to the harmonies of mooing cows, on my way to the interesting community of Janesville. A rancher, mending fences, stops long enough to shake his head and comment on my drawing: "Well, that's another way to earn a living, I guess."

Split rail fence near Susanville, Lassen County

The Genesee-Beckwourth Road

In Genesee Valley I find idyllic farm scenery with grazing cows and sheep, old barns, and old farms. There is still a good collection of buildings marking the former hamlet of Genesee. I continue on Beckwourth Road, crossing a creek full of big granite boulders at Drum Bridge. The landscape changes dramatically farther along when great lava outcroppings appear. The forest becomes sparse, and gray-green sagebrush patterns the landscape. I come across horses in the road. Then deer and fawns leap across the way.

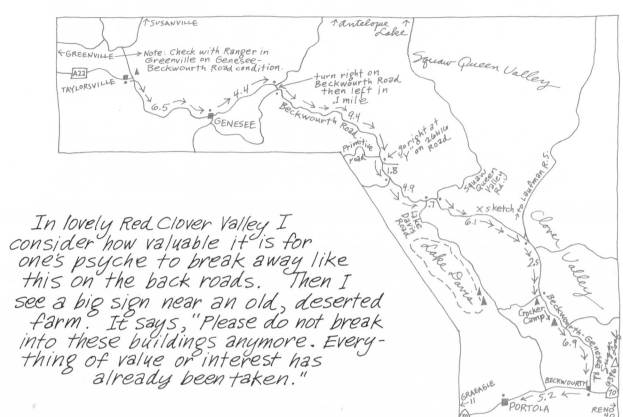

In lovely Red Clover Valley I
consider how valuable it is for
one's psyche to break away like
this on the back roads.   Then I
see a big sign near an old, deserted
farm. It says, "Please do not break
into these buildings anymore. Every-
thing of value or interest has
already been taken."

I despair that
a sign like
this is necessary.
I then must
rationalize that
the people who
buy my book and
travel this road are
those with a genuine feeling for
history and nature who would protect what they see.
       I pass meadows with cows lying contentedly in them.
There is no fencing. I view the striking Sugar Loaf
Mountain and finally reach Beckwourth and Highway 70.
Jim Beckwourth, trapper and scout, was the first to
   locate Beckwourth Pass, at 5,212 feet the lowest
over the summit of the Sierras.
       The Masonic Temple building is still standing
in Beckwourth. There is also a general store
   and the colorful Beckwourth Tavern interior.

Red Clover Valley, Plumas County

102

Johnsville, Plumas County

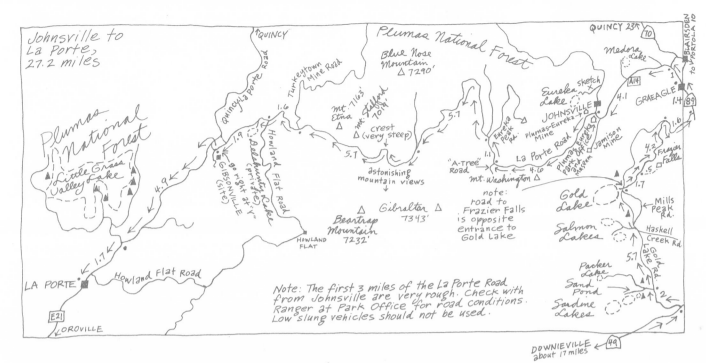

Note: The first 3 miles of the La Porte Road from Johnsville are very rough. Check with Ranger at Park Office for road conditions. Low slung vehicles should not be used.

The Johnsville Road to La Porte

I travel Gold Lake Road to the fabled lake whose shoreline was supposedly covered with chunks of gold. This was according to a J.R. Stoddard, who had stumbled across such a lake, he said, somewhere between Downieville and Sierra Valley in 1849. It was never found, yet the name Gold Lake was given to this lovely body of water.

I take the road opposite the lake to Frazier Falls. A ½-mile hike takes me to a good view of the 248-foot cascade of water. Graeagle is close by and so are the old mining town of Johnsville and Plumas-Eureka State Park.

I stop to draw Johnsville and Mount Washington from the road to Eureka Lake. At the park museum are Snowshoe Thompson's 25-pound skis, which he used to carry the mail across the Sierras in wintertime. He did this for five years beginning in 1856, skiing from Placerville to Carson Valley, Nevada, and back. After a visit to the museum, I inspect portions of the nearby Plumas-Eureka mine, where millions of dollars in gold were produced.

"The first three miles are the bumpiest," I am told by the ranger at the State Park, as we discuss the road to La Porte. He's right. I drive at much less than ten miles per hour. I listen to a classical music station beaming Beethoven's Emperor concerto from Reno, Nevada. My spirit is filled with the beauty of it all. It should never be made an easier trip. I finally reach the crest of this high Sierra journey—a bit steep but maneuverable—and later pass the site of Gibsonville town on the road to La Porte.

103

Oroville to Feather
Falls and Milsap Bar
(map, page 106)

The town of Feather
Falls is attractively
unified in design with
each building painted
barn red with white
trim. Proceeding toward
Milsap Bar along a
particularly dusty stretch
of road, a man astride
a small motorcycle
approaches. He slows and
I slow to minimize dust.
He stops. I stop. We chat
in the middle of the road.
He is the friendly owner
of the Cascade Saloon, and
I am intrigued enough by his description
of the place to locate and draw it.
It is 19 miles to a telephone from here
and there is no electricity. The beer is
quite cold, however, for there is plenty of
bottled gas to keep the power going. I watch
bumblebees in the flower garden, have a
beer, and sit in the shade of a colossal
cedar tree to draw. There is camping here
and at Milsap Bar.
At Milsap the water of the Feather
River looks invitingly cool on a hot
summer day as it flows around
great granite boulders and churns
down the canyon.

Cascade Saloon,
Cascade, Plumas County

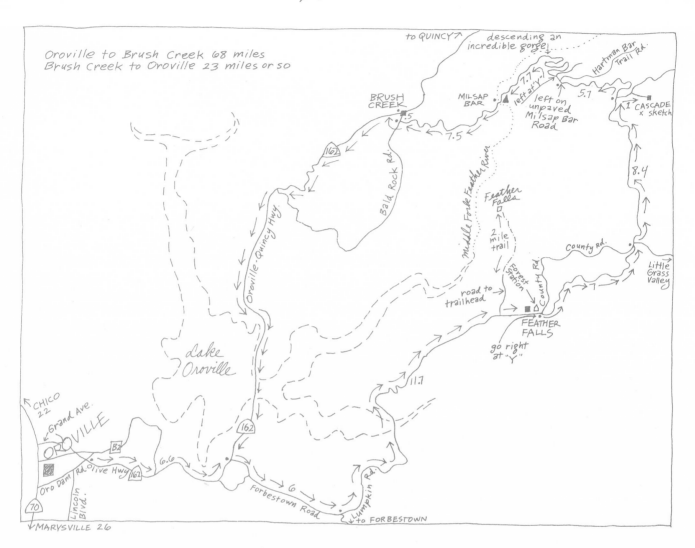

Oroville to Brush Creek 68 miles
Brush Creek to Oroville 23 miles or so

to QUINCY

descending an
incredible gorge!

Hartman Bar
Trail Rd.

7.7

MILSAP
BAR

left at "y"

5.7

left on
unpaved
Milsap Bar
Road

1 CASCADE
x sketch

BRUSH
CREEK

.5

7.5

8.4

162

Bald Rock Rd.

Middle Fork Feather River

Oroville-Quincy Hwy.

Feather
Falls

2
mile
trail

County Rd.

Little
Grass
Valley

road to
trailhead

Forest
Station

County Rd.

7

Lake
Oroville

FEATHER
FALLS

go right
at "Y"

CHICO
22

Grand Ave.

OROVILLE

162

11.7

B

162

6.6

162

Oro Dam Rd.

Olive Hwy

6

Forbestown Road

Lumpkin Rd.

to FORBESTOWN

70

Lincoln Blvd.

MARYSVILLE 26

The Garden Highway to Marysville and Yuba City

It is easy to get onto this road by simply coming off Interstate 5 at the Garden Highway sign just north of Sacramento. You are immediately on a levee road along the Feather River. Pay no attention to an official-looking sign, "For Yuba City go back to freeway." You will get to Yuba City on the back roads.

Interesting and sometimes elegant houses line riverbanks screened by huge bushes of oleanders. There are good views of the river from time to time and of the rich farmland of the Sacramento delta region. Plums, walnuts, corn, peaches, and tomatoes are some of the crops planted. I stop along Scheiber Road to sketch one of the great farms, the "Circle S."

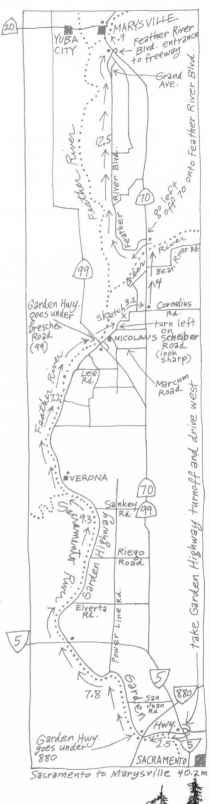

20

MARYSVILLE
YUBA CITY
.9 Feather River Blvd. entrance to freeway
Grand Ave.
12.5
Feather River Blvd.
70
go left off 70 onto Feather River Blvd.
Feather River
99
Bear River
River Rd.
Bear River
.4
Cornelius Rd.
Garden Hwy. goes under Drescher Road (99)
sketch 3.2
X
turn left on Scheiber Road (look sharp)
NICOLAUS
Marcum Road
Lee Rd.
Feather River
7.2
VERONA
Sacramento River
9.3
Sankey Rd.
70
99
Garden Highway
Riego Road
Elverta Rd.
Power Line Rd.
5
5
880
7.8
San Juan Rd.
Garden Hwy.
take Garden Highway turnoff and drive west
Garden Hwy. goes under 880
2.5
5
SACRAMENTO

Sacramento to Marysville 40.2 m

Ranch near Nicolaus, Sutter County

WILLOWS 18 ↑↑ Road 67
PRINCETON ■
take free
ferry to Hwy 45
Road 69
also called
Rd. xx
45
to COLUSA
River Road
Gridley Rd.
15.5
Knights Landing
to Princeton,
59.3 miles
Sacramento River
River Road
turn right
on Bridge St.
Sutter
Buttes
COLUSA ■
Butte Slough Rd.
5.7
Pass Road
45
20
Meridian Rd.
3.6
Mawson Rd.
views of the Buttes
MERIDIAN ■
20 to YUBA CITY
4
So. Drexler Rd.
Moroni Rd.
watch for left
turn on Meridian
go left
on Meridian
Meridian
5.2
Meridian Road
Garmire Road
Acme Rd.
Tisdale Rd.
Sacramento River
Coles Rd.
Knights Landing
to Princeton
59.3 miles
Pelger Rd.
45
24.5
Cranmore Road
Subaco Rd.
Kirkville Rd.
↑ to
WILLIAMS
Seymour Rd.
5
Cranmore Road
to YUBA CITY
113
note: turn left on
Cranmore Rd. just
after crossing the
drawbridge
KNIGHTS
LANDING
E10 9
Road 13
.8
113 E8
to
WOODLAND
8.5 ↓
Rd. 102
8.5
↓ to
5

Crossing the Sacramento River at Princeton,
Colusa County

*Knights Landing to
Princeton Ferry along
the Sacramento River*

Knights Landing, where scenes
were filmed around 1929 for
the movie SHOWBOAT, begins
this drive along the levee
roads of the Sacramento River.
Levee roads offer views of both
the river and agricultural land.
I watch tomatoes being harvested.
Occasionally, trucks would spill some at a
turn in the road and the blood-red squashed fruit looked
like a mortal wound in the pavement.
Blue and white herons watch me pass. Scores of
dragonflies dodge my car. Later I get a good view of
Sutter Buttes, the unusual little mountain range in the
center of the Sacramento Valley where John C.
Fremont camped in 1846. There are walnut and
peach orchards and more levees to ride on the
way to the Princeton Free Ferry.

Wheatland to Smartville

Annual grasses make up much of the vegetation in this rolling Sierra foothill country. The road passes through the Spenceville Wildlife Area, most glorious when clad in the green of spring.
Classic groves of blue, live, and valley oaks decorate the hillsides. Seated among old headstones in a hillside cemetery on McGanny Lane, I draw a view of the hamlet of Smartville. It is at Smartville that I begin to feel the atmosphere of California's gold country. The 1870 church is still the most prominent building in town and at the top of O'Brien Street is the old frame Masonic Temple.

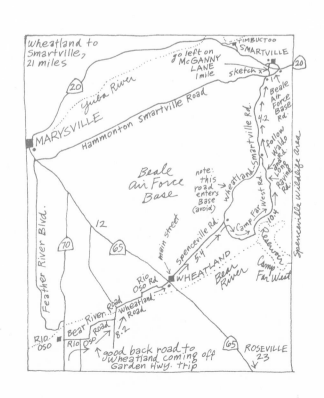

View of Smartville, Yuba County

111

Roundabout to Nevada City

Bitney Springs Road winds through the hills above the active, growing town of Grass Valley. At Bridgeport is the longest covered bridge (233 feet) in America. It spans the South Fork of the Yuba River. In 1862, when the bridge was erected, Bridgeport was a prosperous river mining town.

At French Corral I sketch the old 1850 Wells Fargo Express Office. Today a lone goat grazes alongside the iron-doored, shuttered office that once guarded millions of dollars in gold.

FRENCH CORRAL

Grass Valley to
Nevada City
37.5 miles

↑ CAMPTONVILLE 8

NORTH COLUMBIA

NORTH SAN JUAN

2.6

Oak Tree Rd.

(49)

2.5

Middle Yuba River

SWEETLAND

Blind Shady Rd.

red iron
bridge over
the Yuba

Purdon Rd.

2

BIRCHVILLE

7.6

Birchville Rd.

Tyler Foote Crossing

Murphy Rd.

1.7

road not good
in wet
weather

FRENCH
CORRAL
sketch x

stay to
left
on Purdon
after passing
Blind Shady
Road

5.6

to ↓ Interstate 80, 27 miles

South Yuba River

2.4

Lake Vera
Purdon Rd.

N. Bloomfield Rd.

20

2.3

cross river, turn
left to see
Bridgeport Covered
Bridge

5.4

NEVADA
CITY

Pleasant Valley Road

49

sketch

North
Bloomfield
Lake Vera Road

Bitney Springs Road

8.6

NEWTON

4 49

20

Hwy.
20

20

3

↓ SMARTVILLE 12.5

GRASS VALLEY

49 ↓ AUBURN 24

The first settler here was, as you might suppose, a
Frenchman who built a corral for his mules in 1849.
There is little left to suggest the large, active
mining community that grew here soon after
the discovery of gold in the area.
     The road to Purdon Crossing over the South
Yuba River wouldn't be one to take in wet
weather. I travel it at 10 miles per hour
and cross the boulder-strewn Yuba on an
old, but decorative, red iron bridge.

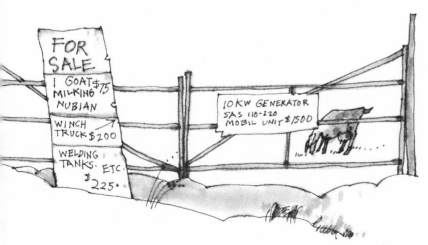

FOR SALE

1 GOAT $75
MILKING
NUBIAN

WINCH
TRUCK $200

10 KW GENERATOR
SAS 110-220
MOBIL UNIT $1500

WELDING
TANKS. ETC.
$225.

French Corral, Nevada County

In Nevada City there is much
to draw of historical interest.
I choose to draw the more than
100-year-old Mulloy house. It
still stands proudly at the
head of — and as you will
discover — in the middle of
Broad Street. Mulloy
had been part owner
of the Nevada
Gazette, as well as
a grocer, a
Justice of the
Peace, and a
county supervisor.

The house on Broad Street,
Nevada City, Nevada County

Nevada City to North Bloomfield and Washington

At Malakoff Diggins, before reaching North Bloomfield, I view the multicolored, pinnacled minarets of earth left by man's attempt to wash away mountains for gold. In the 1870s hydraulic mining was used to find gold that panning, cradles, and long toms couldn't uncover.

Malakoff Diggins, Nevada County

Farmers objected to all the debris carried downstream
by the ruthless procedure, and in 1884 — in a court
case that received wide attention — Judge Lorenzo
Sawyer handed down a ruling that would control
future hydraulic mining in California. Millions of
dollars in gold undoubtedly still lie in
those mountains.

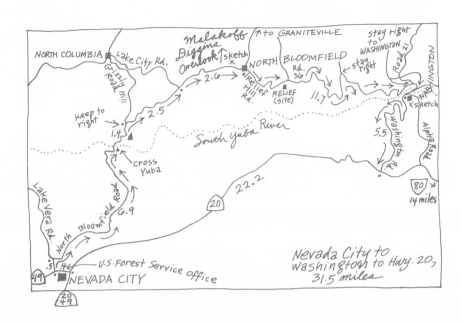

Nevada City to
Washington to Hwy. 20,
31.5 miles

North Bloomfield is a shaded community of old, well-kept houses and historic buildings, maintained by the Park Service. At Washington I sketch the general store. I notice three small hotels here and a restaurant, and I learn that the siren atop the general store goes off on Mondays at noon (unless the siren person forgets).

General store, Washington, Nevada County

North Bloomfield to Graniteville
and across the Sierras
(map, page 122)

Graniteville, at 4,900 feet elevation,
is in the High Sierras. Gold was
mined in gulches here as far back
as 1850, but after 1883 its
existence depended on quartz
mining and lumbering. Today it
is a peaceful community where
residents appreciate a quiet and
simple life in a remote and
beautiful place. I stop to draw
and to talk to the owners of the
1859 house that had been the
residence of the local judge.
   A cedar and a ponderosa pine,
planted in front in 1895, have since
grown to dwarf the old house.
Very few trees were here at
that time because the lumber of the
area had been used up for housing
and mine timber.
   The only road going east out
of Graniteville takes me to
Bowman Lake, Jackson Meadow
Reservoir, and, finally, to
Highway 89. I realize I have
crossed the mighty Sierras
on a back road!

The Judge's Place, Graniteville, Nevada County

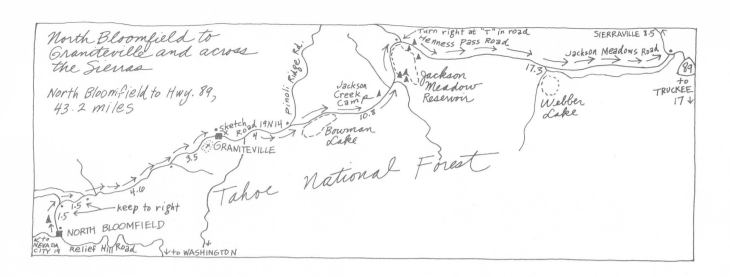

North Bloomfield to Graniteville and across the Sierras

North Bloomfield to Hwy. 89, 43.2 miles

Pinoli Ridge Rd.

Turn right at "T" in road
Henness Pass Road

SIERRAVILLE 8.5

Jackson Meadows Road

17.3

89
to
TRUCKEE
17 ↓

sketch Road 19N14
4
GRANITEVILLE
3.5

Jackson Creek Camp

Jackson Meadow Reservoir

Bowman Lake

10.8

Webber Lake

Tahoe National Forest

4.6

1.5
keep to right

1.5

NORTH BLOOMFIELD

← to NEVADA CITY 19
Relief Hill Road
↓ to WASHINGTON

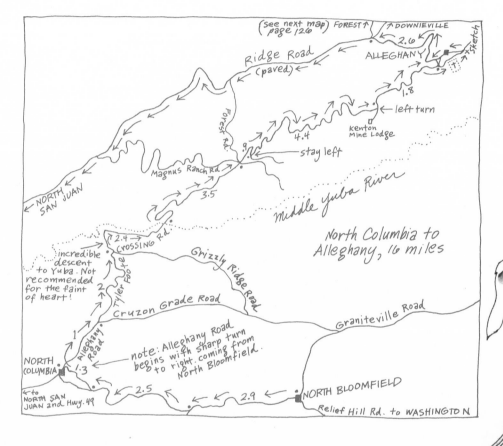

(see next map) FOREST ↑
page 126

↗ DOWNIEVILLE
2.6
ALLEGHANY
sketch

Ridge Road
(paved) ←

1.8
← left turn

Forest Rd.

4.4
Kenton Mine Lodge

.9
stay left

Magnus Ranch Rd.

3.5

NORTH SAN JUAN ←

Middle Yuba River

North Columbia to Alleghany, 16 miles

2.4
CROSSING RD.

Grizzly Ridge Road

incredible descent to Yuba. Not recommended for the faint of heart!

Tyler Foote Rd.

2

Cruzon Grade Road

Graniteville Road

1

Alleghany Road

NORTH COLUMBIA

1.3

note: Alleghany Road begins with sharp turn to right coming from North Bloomfield.

← to NORTH SAN JUAN and Hwy. 49

2.5 ←

2.9 ←

NORTH BLOOMFIELD

Relief Hill Rd. to WASHINGTON

North Columbia to Alleghany back road

I pick the old A.D. Foote toll road to reach Alleghany. It seems incredible that men would build such a road, hewn out of rock and threading its way along a nearly perpendicular canyon wall. At several turns, walls of dry masonry are observed supporting sections of precipitous roadway.

122

At the beginning of the journey it is somewhat intimidating to find a sign, "Narrow road, no turnouts, one lane, last turnaround." I make it, however, sometimes at a bumpy 5 miles per hour. I ford the Yuba at Footes Crossing, drive on for big views of canyons and mountains, and eventually reach the High Sierra town of Alleghany. It is strung out along the mountainside in picturesque fashion. I sit to draw the tiny fire department in this colorful town of shiny, sloping metal roofs. From here it is easy to return to Highway 49 for the road is paved and there are more good views of forests and mountains to enjoy. This is the old Henness Pass Road, the main emigrant trail in 1849 leading from Virginia City, Nevada, to Marysville.

ALLEGHANY USPS FIRE TOOL CACHE

NO PARKING ANY TIME

ALLEGHANY FIRE DEPT

Alleghany Fire Department

Alleghany to Forest, Camptonville or Downieville

In the middle 1850s Forest was a lively mining camp.
When it became a town it was named for a Mrs. Mooney,
a newspaperwoman with the unlikely first name of
Forest. She signed her journalistic efforts, "Forest City."
    I arrive in Forest to find a small, quiet alpine
community. Opposite the Ruby Mine Office, operators
of nearby gold mines, I sit under an apple tree to
draw. Behind the office, in the gully, is the
    entrance to a caved-in mining tunnel. When
miles of tunnels were being worked here, one could
go all the way to Alleghany without worrying about
    the winter snow. Forest and Alleghany were
connected by all the mining tunnels!

RUBY MINE
OFFICE

House at Forest, Sierra County

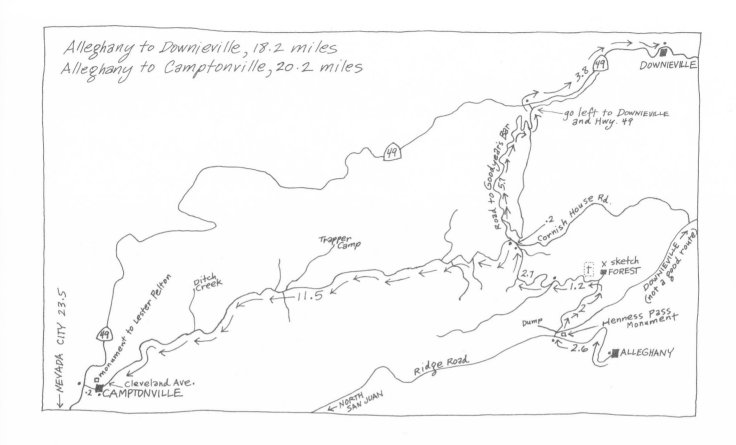

Alleghany to Downieville, 18.2 miles
Alleghany to Camptonville, 20.2 miles

DOWNIEVILLE

3.8 49

go left to DOWNIEVILLE
and Hwy. 49

49

Road to Goodyear's Bar

5.7

.2   Cornish House Rd.

Trapper
Camp

Ditch
Creek

x sketch
FOREST

DOWNIEVILLE → (not a good route)

2.1

1.2

→.2

11.5

NEVADA CITY 23.5

monument to Lester Pelton

Dump

Henness Pass
Monument

Ridge Road

← 2.6   ■ ALLEGHANY

49

Cleveland Ave.

.2 ■ CAMPTONVILLE

← NORTH
SAN JUAN

I then travel to the charming, historic town of
Downieville via Goodyear's Bar, a winding mountain
road, narrow, steep, and rough. I get a strong
impression of the tremendous dimension and
depth of these canyons of the High Sierras.
    An easier route, yet with grand mountain views,
is the road to Camptonville. Named for a blacksmith,
Robert Campton, the little town is noted as the place
where Lester Pelton invented the Pelton
Water Wheel in 1878.

Back road, Mourning Dove,
Sierra County

127

Northern California

FAIRFIELD ■ Rio Vista to Freeport → ■ SACRAMENTO

101

12 RIO VISTA

Sherman, Twitchell and Tyler roads

■ LODI

5 99

Road through Montezuma Hills

Levee road to Tracy

■ STOCKTON

580 TRACY

■ PATTERSON

SAN JOSE ■

Road to Lick Observatory

Farm Roads to Gustine

101

Back road from Gilroy

■ GUSTINE

GILROY ■

Roads to Dos Palos

■ MERCED

LOS BANOS ■

152

■ DOS PALOS

Dos Palos to Kingsburg

5

SOLEDAD ■

FRESNO ■

The road through Arroyo Seco Canyon

■ KING CITY

■ KINGSBURG

JOLON ■

King City back roads

Indian Valley and Peach Tree Roads

Farm roads of the east San Joaquin

PASO ROBLES ■

Paso Robles back roads

DELANO ■

Southern California

Pacific Ocean

Central California

Nevada

Eucalyptus, Santa Cruz County

Central California

With some good maps and an extra bit of time,
  I set off — still with a sense of adventure
in taking a back route and coming upon
  the unexpected.
    I believe we all need to express
our appreciation of beauty. What better
  way to fulfill this need than by
getting closer to nature on the
    back roads.

The road through Montezuma Hills (map, page 133)

Along Shiloh Road the land is rolling. Occasional eucalyptus trees bend in the wind. I pass through Birds Landing, a shipping point for hay and wheat in the 1870s. The old Benjamin Store (1875) still stands. Almost forgotten, Collinsville hamlet slumbers at the river's edge, where the San Joaquin joins the Sacramento. The handsome profile of Mount Diablo is outlined across the water. Long ago Collinsville was a salmon fishing village. The many fishermen from Italy who worked in the cannery lived in houses built on stilts to allow flood tides to pass beneath. The town was referred to as "Little Venice."

Farm near Birds Landing, Solano County

Cows, sheep, flocks of crows, hawks, lonely farms, and lonelier windmills are seen while driving through the Montezuma Hills from Birds Landing.
    The road to Rio Vista curves among the summer golden hills of Montezuma.

In town, at the corner of California and 4th streets, I draw St. Joseph's Church, built in 1868. It is surrounded by concrete painted green. From where I sketch the concrete looks like grass.

St. Joseph's Church, Rio Vista, Solano County

Sherman, Brannan, Twitchell, and Tyler

There are meandering levee roads off Highway 160 beginning with Sherman Island Road, which follows the broad San Joaquin River, then Three Mile Slough. Brannon Island Road and Twitchell Island Road bring views of corn, grain, and hay crops on the land side, boats and water skiers on the water side.

Fairfield to Collinsville
to Rio Vista, 37.9 miles
Antioch to Walnut Grove on
delta island back roads, 46.1 miles
Rio Vista to Freeport, 30.4 miles

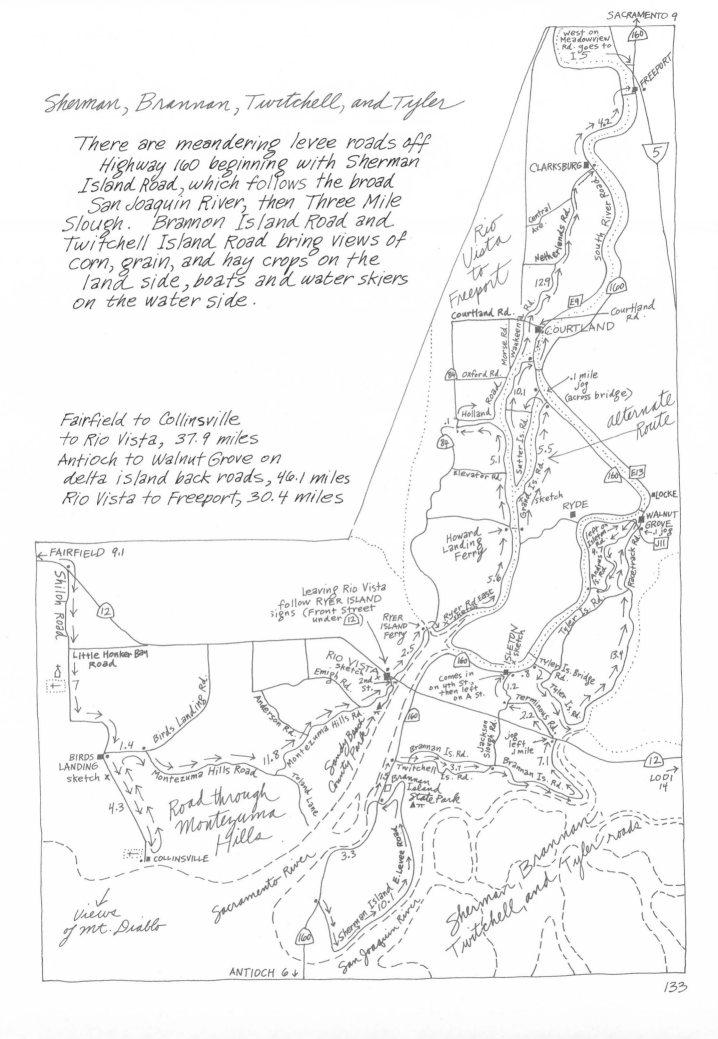

City Hall, Rio Vista, Solano County

The towering dredge moored at Isleton is the town's
most prominent feature. I sketch the City Hall as
the siren blows and volunteer firemen rush to duty
adjusting their suspenders as they go. A small town
is not without drama. I complete my meandering with
a drive around Tyler Island, which brings me.
again to Highway 160

Rio Vista to Clarksburg and Freeport (map, page 133)

I find Rio Vista a clean, pleasant riverside town. An attractive marina is nearby and a county park for camping and picnicking along the Sacramento River.
I stopped to see the Dutra Museum of Dredging. The Dutra family have made their lovely 1907 house into a comprehensive and significant presentation of the history of dredging in the Delta region.
I sketch a huge bucket used on the dredge Tule King, constructed in 1910. Its 25,000 pounds tower over the family cat in the Dutra backyard.
Phone 707-374-5015 for an appointment to see the museum.

Tule King dredge bucket, Rio Vista, Solano County

Going north I ride the free ferry
to Ryer Island and sketch a well-proportioned
sailboat docked in Hidden Harbor.
    The day is quiet and bird sounds predominate.
Geese pose in the water. A commercial crayfisher-
man speaks to me. His 150 traps are inspected
daily in the warm summer months. One sardine and a
can of dogfood are used as bait in each trap. His
take in one trap can be anywhere from one to one
hundred crayfish. Once hauled in, the crayfish
are frozen and shipped to Sweden, where they
are most particularly relished.

Delta boat, Ryer Island, Sacramento County

137

An alternate route, Rio Vista to Courtland and Freeport
(map, page 133)

This road differs from the previous road in that a second free ferry at Howard Landing takes you onto Grand Island, then north again toward Freeport. Along this route, Sutter Island and Merritt Island are also traversed. On Grand Island I draw a fine Victorian house along Steamboat Slough.

House on Steamboat Slough, Yolo County

I ride the levees, eventually arriving in Freeport, once a major shipping center for the gold mines. A.J. Bump built the first general store/saloon in town in 1863. It is still there when I arrive on a warm summer day in July; a cool drink at the colorful, old saloon tastes good. (map, page 133)

Levee road to Tracy

Strange as it seems, there are numerous islands right in the center of California. Flood plains of the Sacramento and San Joaquin rivers, reclaimed over the years for agriculture, created the many islands.
Riding levee roads requires a sharp eye. all around. The levees give a command position for appreciating the waterways and the special look of island agriculture.
I sketch a historic country schoolhouse off Inland Road. It was built in 1904 and abandoned in 1946.

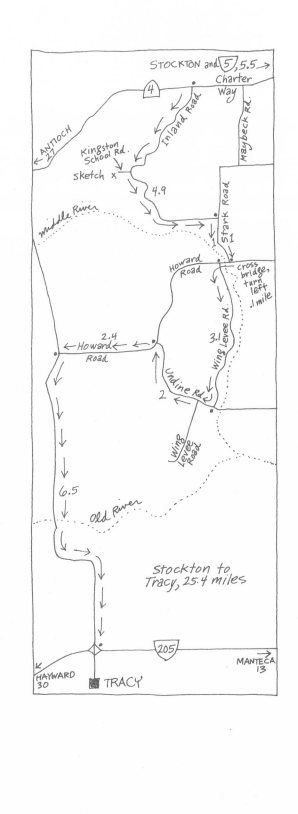

STOCKTON and 5 5.5 →

Charter Way

ANTIOCH 27 ←

4

Inland Road

Maybeck Rd.

Kingston School Rd.

sketch x

4.9

middle River

Stark Road

1 1

Howard Road

cross bridge, turn left .1 mile

3.1

Wing Levee Rd.

2.4 ← Howard Road ←

Undine Rd.

2

Wing Levee Road

6.5

Old River

Stockton to Tracy, 25.4 miles

205

HAYWARD 30 ←

TRACY

MANTECA 13 →

Kingston School,
San Joaquin County

141

The road
to Lick
Observatory
and San Antonio
Valley

It is a windy day and overcast with thick, dark clouds.
The still green hills have begun to turn brown in some
areas. Wildflowers are cheerful spots of color on this
gray day. I stop to draw a view of Lick Observatory—
framed with oaks—visible along the ridge of Mount
Hamilton. As I drive the winding road, ground squirrels
scurry back and forth to their burrows in the bases of
ancient oak trees. You can see the mighty 120"
telescope any day of the week, and from one to five p.m. a
film may be seen at the Visitors' Center.

Lick Observatory, Mount Hamilton, Santa Clara County

It is 50 miles from here to Livermore on Lick Observatory
Road, which winds down the east side of Mount Hamilton
and through the lovely oak meadows of San Antonio Valley.
Here the road divides, going north to Livermore
and east to Patterson.

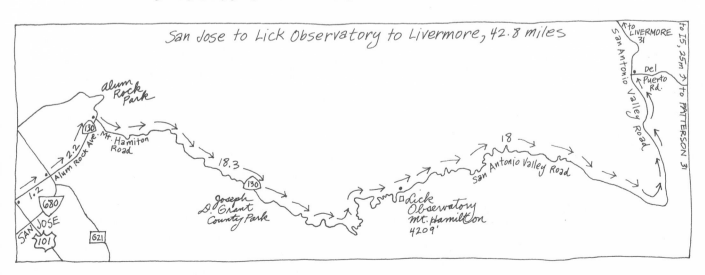

San Jose to Lick Observatory to Livermore, 42.8 miles

Alum Rock Park

130

2.2

Alum Rock Ave. · Mt. Hamilton Road

1.2

680

SAN JOSE

101

621

18.3

130

Joseph D. Grant County Park

Lick Observatory Mt. Hamilton 4209'

18

San Antonio Valley Road

San Antonio Valley Road

Del Puerto Rd.

to LIVERMORE 31

to I5, 25m → to PATTERSON 31

Back road from Gilroy

The town of Gilroy was named
for John Gilroy, soapmaker and
millwright. He had married the
daughter of Ygnacio Ortega, owner
of Rancho San Ysidro, and was given part
of the Rancho (4,460 acres) when Ygnacio
died in 1833.

La Cañada Ranch, near Gilroy,
Santa Clara County

145

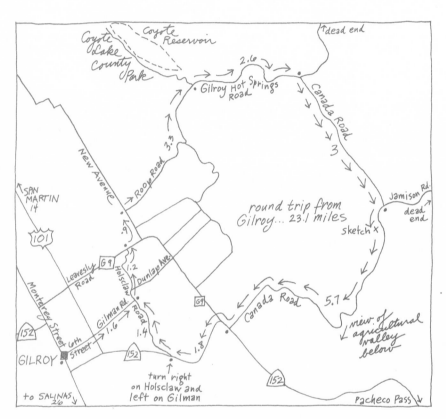

Back road mailbox

John was influential enough for the present town
of Gilroy to be named for him; however, in 1869 he died
in poverty, aged 73 years. It is interesting that his
name was really Cameron. Gilroy was his mother's
maiden name, which he took when he deserted
ship at Monterey in 1814 so as not to be traced.
   I sketch a scene along Canada Road, a ranch
nestled at the base of sloping hills. Poppies, mustard,
and purple vetch bloom on this bright spring day.
   I watch a bobcat warily cross the road
   and bound through grass and flowers.

The road through Arroyo Seco Canyon

I see the harvesting of lettuce on my way. A huge motorized sprinkler creeps over the planted landscape of cabbage, onions, and grape crops. One large unplanted field is orange with poppies.

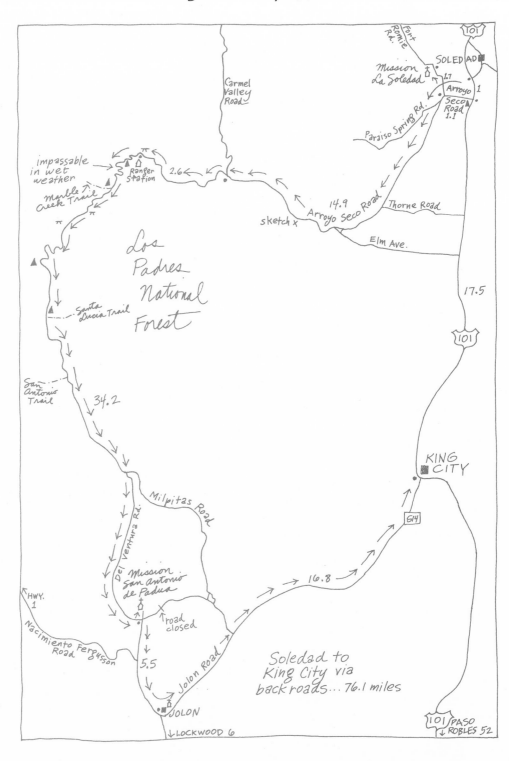

Carmel Valley Road

Fort Romie Rd.

101

SOLEDAD

Mission La Soledad

1.7

Arroyo Seco Road 1.1

1

Paraiso Spring Rd.

impassable in wet weather

Ranger Station

2.6

14.9

Arroyo Seco Road

Thorne Road

sketch x

Elm Ave.

Marble Creek Trail

17.5

101

Los Padres National Forest

Santa Lucia Trail

San Antonio Trail

34.2

KING CITY

Milpitas Road

Del Ventura Rd.

G14

16.8

Mission San Antonio de Padua

HWY. 1

road closed

Nacimiento Fergusson Road

5.5

Jolon Road

Soledad to King City via back roads...76.1 miles

JOLON

↓LOCKWOOD 6

101/PASO ↓ROBLES 52

147

I draw a white barn and the complex canyon walls of Arroyo Seco, while the ranch dog returns a large rock for me to throw again and again.

Gould Ranch, Arroyo Seco Canyon, Monterey County

It is April, and with forest fires unlikely and the temperature comfortable, an ideal time to travel this colorful road. The road ends at Mission San Antonio de Padua, founded in 1771 and one of the most picturesque of the California missions. It stands in the valley of the San Antonio River and had been well known for its high quality wheat and fine horses.

The road narrows in Los Padres National Forest and winds along mountain ledges. Yucca blooms in creamy white splendor, and firewood, ceanothus, monkey flower, paintbrush, and yerba santa color the roadside.

Grapevine in May, near King City,
Monterey County

King City back roads

On Oasis Road I see thousands of grapevines patterning the hills and dales south of King City. They are all marked, cordoned, and prepared for mechanical harvesting. I draw an Early Burgundy varietal at the flowering stage when young grape bunches are just beginning. A sprinkling device is attached to this grape stake. An airplane is dusting other vineyards in the vicinity with sulphur, but I am lucky to be distant enough from this activity.

The roads parallel Highway 101 and I find myself south of San Ardo surrounded by a forest of oil pump jacks. I hold my nose and clear this area as I proceed inland on Sargeants Valley Road. Brown rolling hills and golden grain fields fill the landscape.

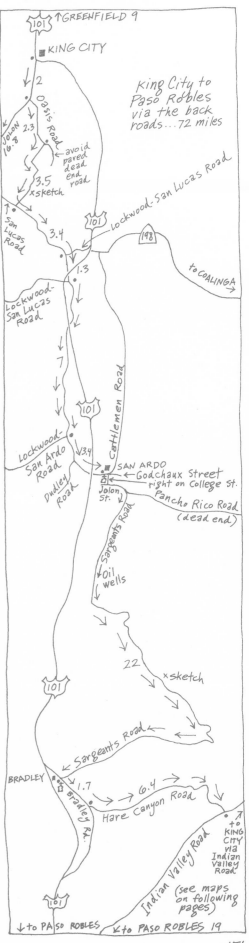

King City to Paso Robles via the back roads...72 miles

101 ↑GREENFIELD 9

■ KING CITY

↓ 2

Oasis Road

Jolon 16.8   2.3

←avoid paved dead end road

↓ 3.5   ×sketch

San Lucas Road

101   3.4   Lockwood-San Lucas Road

198   to COALINGA →

Lockwood-San Lucas Road   1.3

7

101

Lockwood-San Ardo Road   ↓3.4

Cattlemen Road

SAN ARDO ■   ← Godchaux Street right on College St.

Dudley Road   Jolon St.   Pancho Rico Road (dead end)

Sargeants Road

↓Oil wells

22   ×sketch

101

Sargeants Road

BRADLEY   1.7   6.4

Bradley Rd.   Hare Canyon Road

Indian Valley Road   to KING CITY via Indian Valley Road

(see maps on following pages)

101

↓to PASO ROBLES   ↓to PASO ROBLES 19

151

I stop to draw a Pinto horse—
an inspired design for a
mailbox made of welded steel
parts. You can return to
Highway 101 at Bradley or
take Hare Canyon Road
and Indian Valley Road to
King City or Paso Robles.

Pinto mailbox, near Bradley, Monterey County

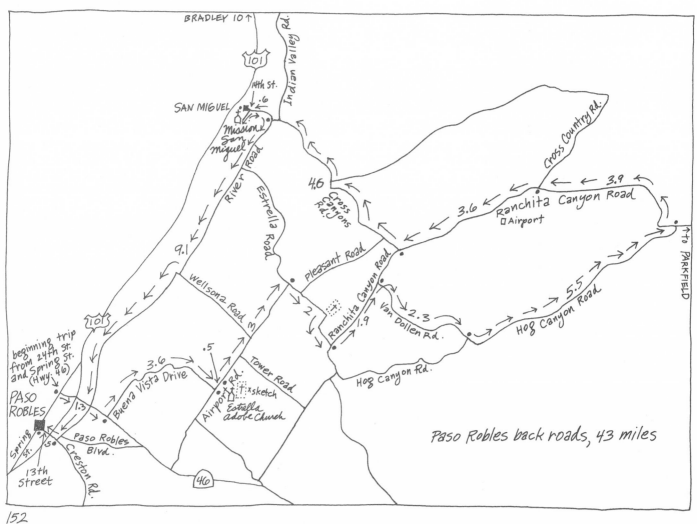

BRADLEY 10 ↑

101

14th St.
.6

SAN MIGUEL

Mission
San
Miguel

River Road

Estrella Road

Indian Valley Rd.

Cross Country Rd.

4.6

Cross
Canyons
Rd.

3.9

3.6

Ranchita Canyon Road

□ Airport

9.1

Pleasant Road

Ranchita Canyon Road

101

Wellsona Road

2

2.3

5.5

1.9

Van Dollen Rd.

Hog Canyon Road

↑to PARKFIELD

beginning trip
from 24th St.
and Spring St.
(Hwy. 46)

3.6

.5

Buena Vista Drive

Tower Road

Hog Canyon Rd.

PASO
ROBLES

1.3

Airport Rd.

×sketch

Estrella
Adobe Church

Spring St.

.5

Paso Robles Blvd.

Creston Rd.

13th
Street

46

Paso Robles back roads, 43 miles

Paso Robles back roads

On the plains of Estrella, in 1879, Christian pioneers built Estrella Adobe Church. It was restored in 1952 and part of the cemetery was saved. From the grave markers, I am able to piece together the heart-tugging story of the Stovall family: Little Albert, the youngest, whose headstone reads "Born May 13, 1881, son died May 4, 1885

Twas our laughing blue eyed Boy.
Our comfort and our household joy
Over the river he beckons to me
The gates of the city we
cannot see";

then the middle son Walter M. (September 8, 1875 - May 23, 1885); mother Mary C. (died March 15, 1905, 63 years 18 days); and father F.M. (died August 16, 1907, 64 years/1 mo./18 dys.).

Evan P.'s marker is pictured here. Sentimental verse has its effect on me!

Roads wind around here and over rolling hills textured with grain, hay crops, and vineyards. A large hawk poses on a fencepost. I stop to explore Mission San Miguel Archangel, a lovely old church founded in 1797, and then return to Paso Robles on River Road.

EVAN P.
SON OF
F. M. & M. C.
STOVALL
BORN
OCT. 30, 1878
DIED
JUNE 15, 1885.

The angels to Evan did whisper,
Jesus ... has called you away,
To join your dear Brothers in Heaven
Our darling did meekly obey.

Headstone at Estrella Adobe Church graveyard, near Paso Robles, San Luis Obispo County

153

Indian Valley and Peach Tree roads

Along Indian Valley and Peach Tree
roads, I see pleasant vistas aplenty of
valleys, farms, rolling hills, majestic oaks,
and pines. Shaded by a giant oak,
I sketch a view of Peach Tree and
Hidalgo canyons looking west into the
late afternoon sun.

On Freeman Flat Road vineyards create
a rolling sea of row upon row of
intensely green vines.

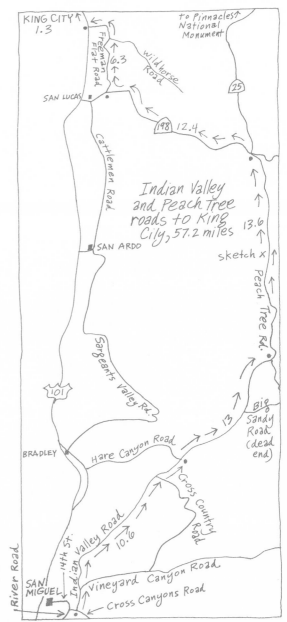

KING CITY
1.3

to Pinnacles
National
Monument

Freeman Flat Road

6.3

Wildhorse Road

SAN LUCAS

25

198   12.4

Cattlemen Road

Indian Valley
and Peach Tree
roads to King
City, 57.2 miles

13.6

sketch x

Peach Tree Rd.

SAN ARDO

Sargeants Valley Rd.

101

Big
Sandy
Road
(dead
end)

13

BRADLEY   Hare Canyon Road

Cross Country Road

14th St.

Indian Valley Road

10.6

River Road

SAN MIGUEL

Vineyard Canyon Road

Cross Canyons Road

Peach Tree Canyon, Monterey County

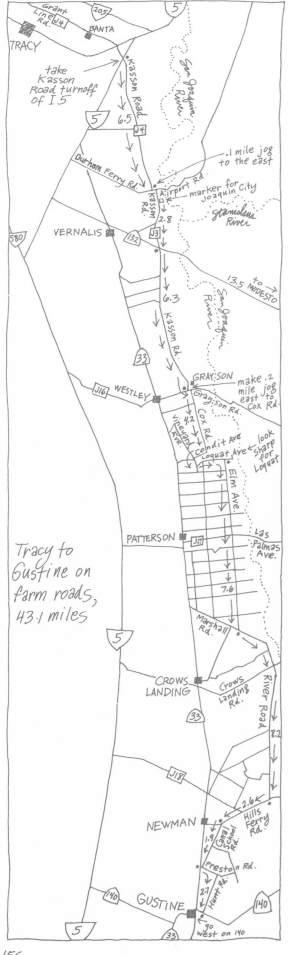

Grant Line J4 Rd.

205

5

BANTA

TRACY

take Kasson Road turnoff of I 5

Kasson Road

San Joaquin River

5

6.5

J4

.1 mile jog to the east

Durham Ferry Rd.

Airport Rd.

marker for San Joaquin City

Kasson Rd.

Stanislaus River

580

VERNALIS

132

J3

2.8

6.3

San Joaquin River

to MODESTO 13.5

Kasson Rd.

33

GRAYSON

make .2 mile jog east to Cox Rd.

J16

WESTLEY

Grayson Rd.

Cox Rd.

4.2

Vineyard Ave.

Condit Ave.

Loquat Ave.

look sharp for Loquat

Elm Ave.

PATTERSON

J17

Las Palmas Ave.

7.6

Tracy to Gustine on farm roads, 43.1 miles

Marshall Rd.

5

CROWS LANDING

Crows Landing Rd.

River Road

33

8.2

J18

2.6

NEWMAN

Hills Ferry Rd.

Canal School Rd.

1.9

Preston Rd.

2.7

Hunt Rd.

140

GUSTINE

140

5

33

go west on 140

Farm roads through the San Joaquin Valley

From Tracy palm-lined Kasson Road goes south, beginning a farm road journey directly through California's greatest agricultural valley. On a clear day the snow-capped Sierras can be viewed to the east. I stop to read a marker at the site of San Joaquin City, established in 1849. In 1880 it had a hotel, warehouse, two saloons, stores, and houses. Pioneers and freight wagons crossed the river at nearby Durham Ferry. The Spanish explorer Gabriel Moraga had named this river San Joaquin in 1813.

Later, I drive around the village of Grayson, noting the many little churches. Along Elm Road I pass a unique enterprise, a turf farm.

In the pleasant town of Gustine, I sketch a small grove of orange trees along its main thoroughfare. Gustine's old-fashioned water tower is in the background. Sighting the water tower is often the first indication of a town in the offing as these farm roads proceed.

Orange trees, Gustine, Merced County

Roads to San Luis Camp and Dos Palos (map, page 160)

A short diversion onto Mercey Springs and Wolfsen roads brings me to San Luis Camp adobe, the oldest building in the county. It was built in 1848 by Francisco Pacheco and became a stopping place for vaqueros driving cattle to the gold fields. When land baron Henry Miller was in the area, he usually stayed here.

Further on I travel through the San Luis Wildlife Refuge. There is a herd of Tule elk in a large enclosure, where one massive-horned bull elk has coraled all the females.

Other bulls stand a long way off, quite deserted and forlorn looking. Some 800 Tule elk are all that remain of the 500,000 that once roamed the grasslands of the San Joaquin Valley. Many ducks, eagles, hawks, and heron are also to be seen in the refuge.

San Luis Camp adobe, Merced County

159

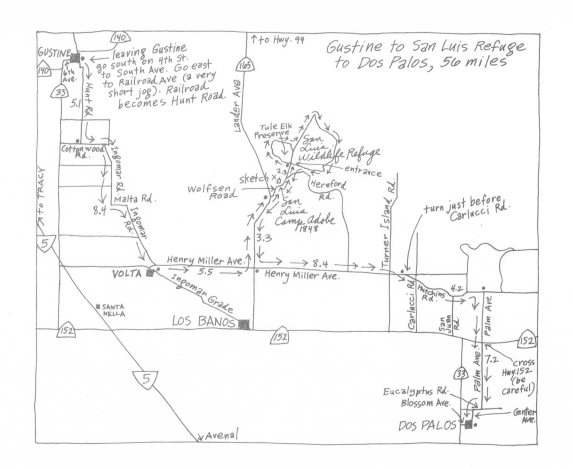

Map labels:
140 — GUSTINE / 6th Ave. / 140 / 33 / Hunt Rd. / 5.1 — leaving Gustine go south on 4th St. to South Ave. Go east to Railroad Ave (a very short jog). Railroad becomes Hunt Road.

↑to Hwy. 99

105 — Lander Ave.

Gustine to San Luis Refuge to Dos Palos, 56 miles

to TRACY — Cottonwood Rd. / Ingomar Rd. / Malta Rd. / 8.4 / Ingomar Rd.

Tule Elk Preserve / San Luis Wildlife Refuge / entrance / 2.3 / sketch X / Wolfsen Road / Hereford Rd. / San Luis Camp Adobe 1848 / 3.3

Turner Island Rd. / turn just before Carlucci Rd.

5 / VOLTA / Ingomar Grade / Henry Miller Ave. / 5.5 / Henry Miller Ave. / 8.4 / Henry Miller Ave.

SANTA NELLA / 152 / LOS BANOS / 152 / 5 / v Avenal

Carlucci Rd. / Hutchins Rd. / 4.2 / San Juan Rd. / Palm Ave. / 152 / 7.2 / cross Hwy. 152 (be careful) / 33 / Palm Ave. / Eucalyptus Rd. / Blossom Ave. / DOS PALOS / Center Ave.

Dos Palos to Kingsburg

In a small brochure called "The Fertile Fields of Dos Palos Colony," published in 1902, farmers were coaxed by landowners Miller and Lux to buy and settle here. Land was $30 to $75 per acre at 6% interest.

Beekeepers realized that in Dos Palos (Two Poles) the rich alfalfa crop aided in creating the thickest, richest, whitest honey in the world. 60,000 dozen eggs a year were produced, alfalfa sold f.o.b. at $8.50 per ton, cows sold for $45 to $60 a head.

Water tower of Dos Palos, Merced County

Two passenger trains as well as two freight trains ran every day to San Francisco, making daily newspapers available. Today Dos Palos continues as a booming agricultural town, center for a large area of diversified farming.

I sketch the new water tower, not as quaint as Gustine's.

On my trip south I see farm roads lined with wads of cotton blown from truck trailers during harvesttime. Big red corn harvesters gather in a winter crop of dried corn and process it; the kernels are then loaded into trucks and carted away.

Nearing Kingsburg, I sketch in the cemetery I remember from my youth, where my mother, dad, and grandparents are buried. It is still a meticulously well-kept place. The cypress trees are even taller than I remember.

Kingsburg itself is a fine valley town with a Swedish theme to its main street (Draper Street) architecture. Reaching Kingsburg, I have now traversed a good part of the San Joaquin Valley on farm roads.

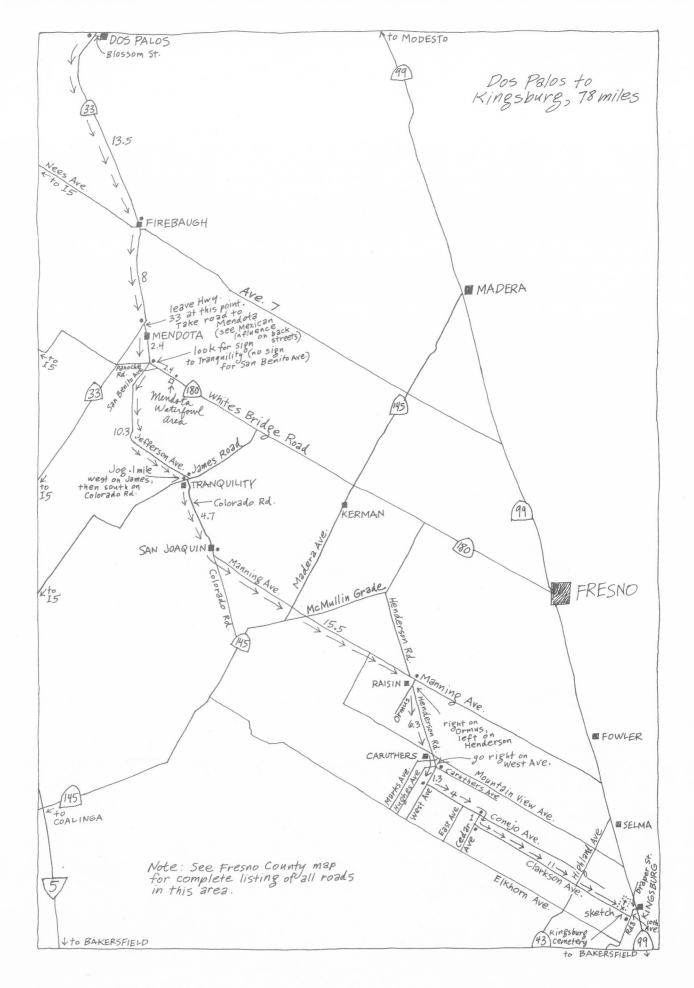

to MODESTO

Dos Palos to
Kingsburg, 78 miles

DOS PALOS
Blossom St.

33

13.5

to MODESTO

99

Nees Ave.
← to I5

FIREBAUGH

MADERA

8

Ave. 7

leave Hwy.
33 at this point.
Take road to
Mendota
(see Mexican
influence on back
streets)

MENDOTA
2.4

look for sign
to Tranquility (no sign
for San Benito Ave.)

←to
I5

Panoche
Rd.

2.4

180

Whites Bridge Road

33

San Benito Ave.

Mendota
Waterfowl
area

145

10.3

Jefferson Ave.   James Road

Jog .1 mile
west on James,
then south on
Colorado Rd.

←to
I5

TRANQUILITY

← Colorado Rd.

KERMAN

4.7

99

Madera Ave.

180

←to
I5

SAN JOAQUIN

Manning Ave.

FRESNO

Colorado Rd.

McMullin Grade

15.5

Henderson Rd.

RAISIN   Manning Ave.

145

Ormus

Henderson Rd.

right on
Ormus,
left on
Henderson

FOWLER

to COALINGA

6.3

CARUTHERS

go right on
West Ave.

Mountain View Ave.

Marks Ave.
Hughes Ave.

Caruthers Ave.

1.3

West Ave.

4

East Ave.

Cedar Ave.

1

Conejo Ave.

SELMA

Highland Ave.

5

Note: See Fresno County map
for complete listing of all roads
in this area.

11

Clarkson Ave.

Elkhorn Ave.

sketch

Draper St.

Rd. 8

KINGSBURG

10th Ave.

↓ to BAKERSFIELD

43

Kingsburg
cemetery

99

to BAKERSFIELD ↓

162

Cypresses, Kingsburg, Fresno County

163

Farm roads of the east San Joaquin Valley

I turn off the busy highway and seek tranquil farm roads going north. I picnic at Lake Woolames on the Friant Kern Canal. Driving on, I see rice and cotton crops, and olive and walnut trees, among many other vegetable and fruit crops. It is raining today and I see cows in muddy splendor near a gigantic pile of manure.

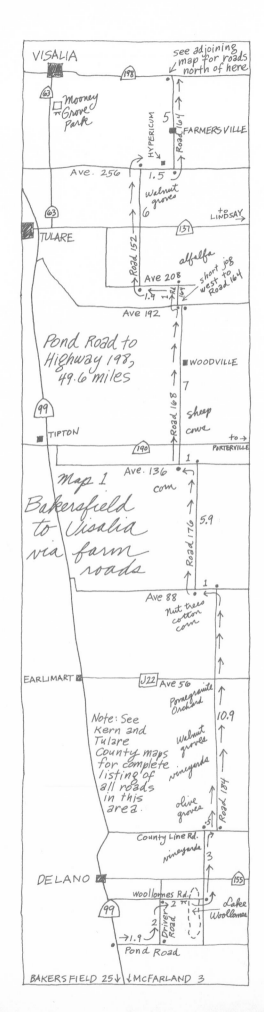

Map 1 — Bakersfield to Visalia via farm roads

VISALIA
198
63
Mooney Grove Park
see adjoining map for roads north of here
5
FARMERSVILLE
HYPERICUM
Road 164
Ave. 256
1.5
63
Walnut groves 6
Road 152
TULARE
137
→ to LINDSAY →
Ave 208
alfalfa
short jog west to Road 164
1.9
Ave 192
Pond Road to Highway 198, 49.6 miles
WOODVILLE
Road 168
7
sheep cows
99
TIPTON
190
→ to PORTERVILLE
1
Ave. 136
corn
Road 176
5.9
1
Ave 88
Nut trees cotton corn
EARLIMART
J22 Ave 56
Pomegranite Orchard
Walnut groves
10.9
vineyards
Road 184
olive groves
.5
County Line Rd.
vineyards
3
DELANO
155
Woollomes Rd.
2 Lake Woollames
Driver Road
2
→ 1.9
Pond Road
BAKERSFIELD 25 ↓   ↓ McFARLAND 3

Note: See Kern and Tulare County maps for complete listing of all roads in this area.

Map 2 — Visalia to Fresno via farm roads

go straight out Shaw → to FRESNO and HWY 99 (20.5 miles)
to ↑ Pine Flat Lake
Highway 198 to Shaw Avenue, 52.1 miles
Shaw Ave.
Ashlan Ave.
Riverbend Ave.
McKinley Ave.
Zediker Ave.
MacDonough Ave.
Floradora Ave.
McKinley Ave.
Viau Ave.
oranges
Trimmer Springs Rd.
1.1
Belmont Ave.
go west on Belmont Rd. for .1 mile, then north on Viau Ave.
1.6
Rio Vista Rd.
King's Canyon Nat. Park
SQUAW VALLEY
1.9
Kings Canyon Rd.
180
63
SANGER
2
Central Ave.
Button Willow Ave.
8 ←
American Ave.
oranges
x sketch
5.9
Anchor Ave.
REEDLEY
lemon groves
4
← Ave 432
olives and oranges
DINUBA
63
Rd 128
6 short jog west, then north again
CUTLER
Rd 144
201
Rd 144
201
Rd 376
4.4
Twin Buttes Δ Δ
Rd. 172
4
Note: See Tulare and Fresno County maps for complete listing of all roads in this area.
Ave. 344 .5
orange groves
99
63
216
6
Rd. 168
VISALIA
.7
198
go over freeway to Rd 168
to TULARE 99 ↓
FARMERSVILLE

Orange groves are
dominant as I proceed
north, skirting foothills
of the Sierra Nevada mountains.
I marvel at how attractively
nature has decorated the
lush green orchard trees
with colorful oranges.

Fresno County oranges

165

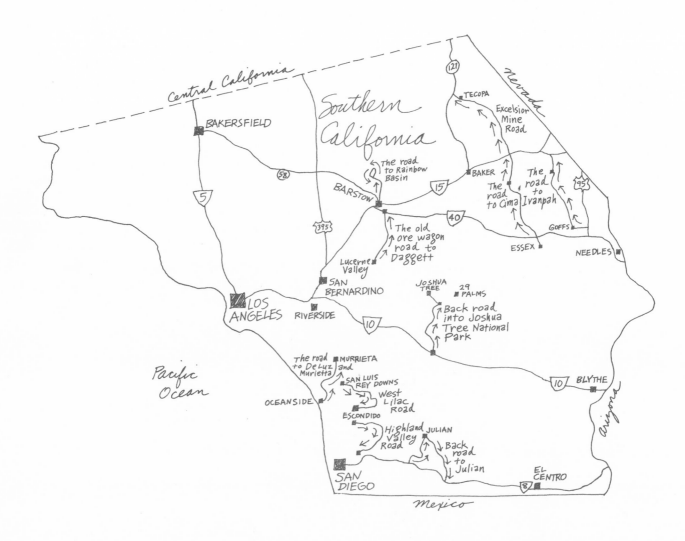

Central California

Southern California

Pacific Ocean

Nevada

Arizona

Mexico

BAKERSFIELD

58

5

395

BARSTOW

The road to Rainbow Basin

15

40

The old ore wagon road to Daggett

Lucerne Valley

SAN BERNARDINO

TECOPA

Excelsior Mine Road

BAKER

The road to Cima

The road to Ivanpah

95

GOFFS

ESSEX

NEEDLES

JOSHUA TREE

29 PALMS

Back road into Joshua Tree National Park

LOS ANGELES

RIVERSIDE

10

The road to DeLuz and Murietta

MURRIETA

SAN LUIS REY DOWNS

West Lilac Road

OCEANSIDE

ESCONDIDO

Highland Valley Road

JULIAN

Back road to Julian

10

BLYTHE

EL CENTRO

8

SAN DIEGO

121

Sketching helps one to see the world through fresh eyes, to see some beauty everywhere, even where it's least expected. Henry Moore said that "one draws to concentrate knowledge."
I believe that this is one of the great functions of drawing. It is a shame that more of us do not take advantage of this avenue of expression to increase our appreciation of the world.
Years ago many more artists and laymen sketched outdoors. They knew well the creative journey the pen takes in the process. The camera has now replaced the pen, I suppose, but without the same rewards.
Knowledge of a subject is not absorbed with the same thoroughness.
It doesn't take long to learn to draw fairly well and I hope you will try it!

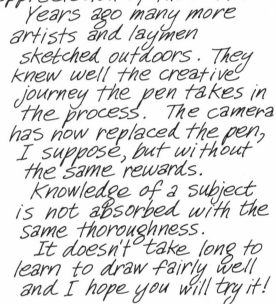

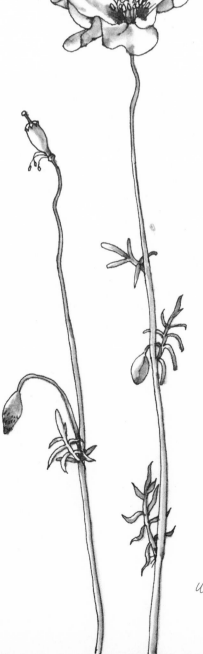

Wind Poppy,
Santa Barbara County

The road to De Luz and Murrieta

Cattle, sheep, and horses once grazed the fields in the valley where Mission San Luis Rey de Francia is located. The church was completed in 1815. Father Peyri, for 34 years the Mission's leader, was forced to leave when a law expelling all Spaniards was passed in 1829. Restoration of the Mission occurred later, and in 1893 it was rededicated as a Franciscan seminary.

Today one must drive a way to outdistance housing and shopping developments that have sprung up in the once secluded valley.

Along North River Road and Sleeping Indian Road, farming country reappears. Strawberry fields cover entire hillsides where scores of laborers pick the fruit. Plastic coverings between the plants glisten like armor plate. Other hills are textured with citrus and avocado groves.

There are palm and eucalyptus
trees, and red tile-roofed
houses perch on knolls in the
picturesque hills.
   Between De Luz and
Murrieta I stop to lunch in
a grove of venerable silver-
barked oaks. Near Murrieta
I am honored with a clear
view of the snowcapped San
Bernardino and San Jacinto
mountains and the broad
valley below.

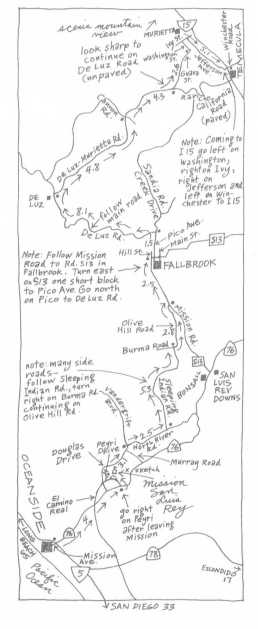

Oceanside to De Luz and Murrieta,
46.6 miles

scenic mountain view
MURIETTA
15
Ivy St.
Winchester Road
TEMECULA
Jefferson Ave.
look sharp to continue on De Luz Road (unpaved)
Washington St.
Guava St.
4.3
Rancho California Road (paved)

Note: Coming to I 15 go left on Washington, right on Ivy, right on Jefferson and left on Winchester to I 15

Cannon Rd.
De Luz-Murietta Rd.
4.8
Sandia Creek Rd.
follow main road
DE LUZ
8.1
De Luz Rd.
Pico Ave.
1.5
Main St.
S13
Hill St.

Note: Follow Mission Road to Rd. S13 in Fallbrook. Turn east on S13 one short block to Pico Ave. Go north on Pico to De Luz Rd.

FALLBROOK
2.5
Mission Rd.
Olive Hill Road
2.8
Burma Road
S13
76

note: many side roads - follow sleeping Indian Rd., turn right on Burma Rd. continuing on Olive Hill Rd.

5.3
Sleeping Indian Rd.
BONSALL
SAN LUIS REY DOWNS

Vanderift Blvd.
2.5
North River Rd.
76

Douglas Drive
Peyri Drive
Murray Road
3.1
sketch
Mission San Luis Rey

El Camino Real
go right on Peyri after leaving Mission

OCEANSIDE
LONG BEACH 65
76
4
Mission Ave.
78
Pacific Ocean
5
ESCONDIDO 17
↓ SAN DIEGO 33

Mission San Luis Rey, San Diego County

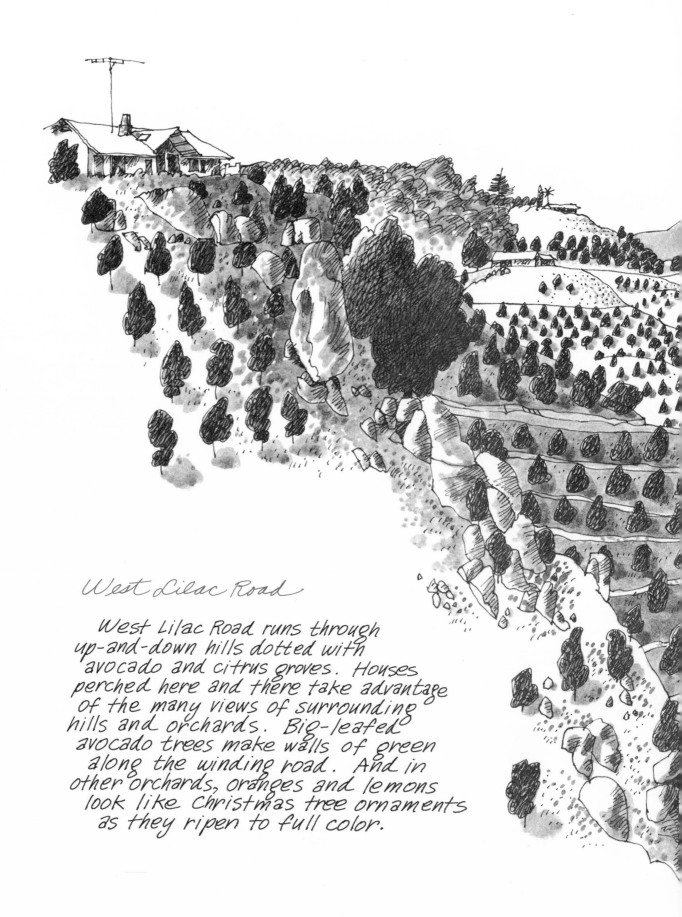

West Lilac Road

West Lilac Road runs through up-and-down hills dotted with avocado and citrus groves. Houses perched here and there take advantage of the many views of surrounding hills and orchards. Big-leafed avocado trees make walls of green along the winding road. And in other orchards, oranges and lemons look like Christmas tree ornaments as they ripen to full color.

avocado orchards, San Diego County

West Lilac Road

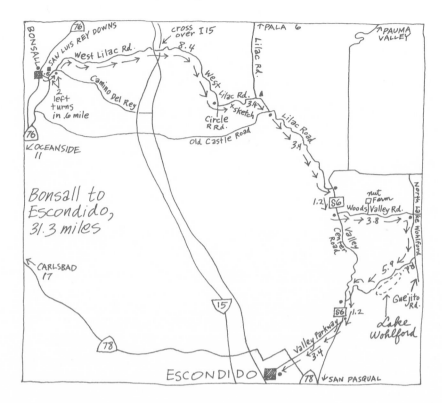

Bonsall to
Escondido,
31.3 miles

Highland Valley Road

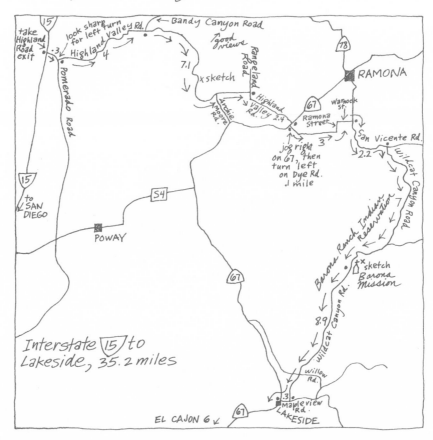

take Highland Road exit

look sharp turn for left Highland Valley Rd.

← Bandy Canyon Road

good views

Rangeland Road

7.1

x sketch

78

RAMONA

Archie Moore Rd.

Highland Valley 2.4

Ramona Street

Warnock St.

67

jog right on 67, then turn left on Dye Rd. .1 mile

3

San Vicente Rd.

2.2

Wildcat Canyon Road

Pomerado Road

Barona Ranch Indian Reservation

x sketch Barona Mission

7

15

to SAN DIEGO

S4

POWAY

67

Wildcat Canyon Rd.

8.9

Interstate [15] to Lakeside, 35.2 miles

Willow Rd.

.3 Mapleview Rd.

EL CAJON 6 ↙

67

LAKESIDE

Highland Valley Road

The avocado trees in my drawing are planted strategically between colossal boulders high above San Pasqual Valley. The two elements seem to complement each other—the dark green trees and the light pink and tan rock formations.

Avocado orchard near Ramona, San Diego County

173

Along the mountain drive through the Barona Indian Reservation, I stop to draw the crisply white Indian Mission. The church has reddish-brown trim with Christmas lights still in place. I inspect the neat, warm interior of the little church and the pictures on the walls. It is a pleasant place indeed. Wildcat Canyon soon descends from here toward Lakeside.

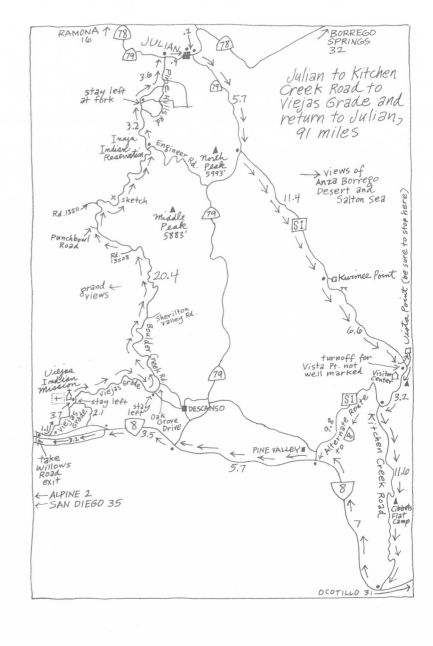

Julian back road round trip

RAMONA ↑ [78]   JULIAN   .2   ↗ BORREGO
16   SPRINGS
[79]   .1   [78]   32
        3.6   Pine Hills Rd.
                                          Julian to Kitchen
stay left   [79]   Creek Road to
at fork   5.7   Viejas Grade and
        3.2   return to Julian,
Inaja   91 miles
Indian   Engineer Rd.   North
Reservation   Peak
                         5993'
                              → views of
Rd.13511   × sketch   Anza Borrego
                    Middle   11.4   Desert and
Punchbowl   Peak   Salton Sea
Road   5883'   [79]
        Rd.   [S1]
        13508
                 20.4   ▪ Kwimee Point
        grand
        views →   6.6
              Sherilton
              Valley Rd.
                                   turnoff for   Visita Point (be sure to stop here)
Viejas   Boulder Creek Rd.   Vista Pt. not
Indian   well marked   Visitor
Mission   Center
        ← stay left   stay   3.2
3.7   2.1   left   [79] DESCANSO   [S1]
    Viejas Grade   Oak   9.8
1.1   Grove   [8]   to   Kitchen Creek Road
        3.2   [8] Drive   ← [8]   Alternate Route
                    3.5   ← PINE VALLEY ▪   11.6
take   5.7
Willows   [8]   Cibbets
Road   Flat
exit   7   Camp
← ALPINE 2
← SAN DIEGO 35
                                   OCOTILLO 31   →

Barona Mission Church,
San Diego County

175

Julian back road round trip

A miner's rush to Julian in 1870 followed the discoverey of gold in the area and lasted until about 1880. Homesteaders followed the miners and fruit growing, bees, and livestock made the town a trading center. Today tourists find its historic atmosphere attractive. I begin from here and travel Highway 79 to Road S1. There are top-of-the-world views along S1 of the great and colorful Desert State Park. Row after row of beige, brown, and pink mountains fade into infinity. Later, descending into Kitchen Valley, I have long views south to the mountains of Mexico. On my return toward Julian Viejas Grade I see a long view of the valley below. Cows graze in the meadows.

I pass Blessed Virgin Mary Church with its colorful cemetery and ascend through brush and rock hills silhouetted against a bright blue sky. Ranches along the road have names like Serenity, Rockin' Chair, Expensive Spread, Fugitive Creek, and Grandpa's Mountains.

I draw a view of Cosmit Peak, which the road semicircles. It is quiet and peaceful here, with a lone circling hawk and an occasional scurrying squirrel.

"Whale" bus, seen along the back roads

View of Cosmit Peak, Boulder Creek Road to Julian, San Diego County

Back road into Joshua Tree National Park

An unmarked back road near Indio heads up a brown and barren canyon that looks quite forbidding. A sign recommends that I have ample gas, oil, and water. A shacklike ranch has another sign stating that attack dogs are on duty. There are rugged, desert hills all around. Possibly this would have been a bandit hideaway in earlier times. As the canyon narrows, I consider that I wouldn't care to be here if flash flooding were a possibility. The road continues to climb. Joshua trees appear and I cross the National Park boundary. There is a sweeping view of Pleasant Valley dotted with Joshua trees.

Malapai Hill, Joshua Tree National Monument, Riverside County

I sketch the black basalt twin peaks of Malapai Hill and drive on to Squaw Tank. Should you begin this trip from within the park, pick up a brochure at the Squaw Tank turnoff of the main drive. Numbered locations are described in it to help you understand the significant geology to be seen. It may be enough, however, to simply observe the masterful arrangement of boulders (as big as houses) set one upon the other and the rich assortment of desert plants: joshuas, yuccas, needle, and cholla cactus, and many more.

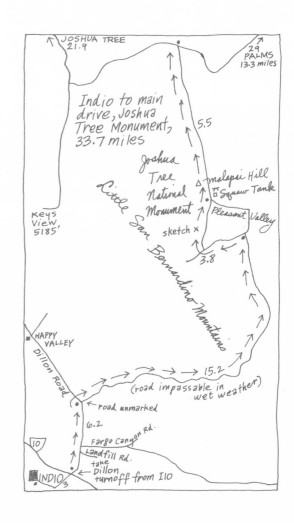

JOSHUA TREE
21.9
29 PALMS
13.3 miles
Indio to main drive, Joshua Tree Monument, 33.7 miles
5.5
Joshua Tree National Monument
Little San Bernardino Mountains
Malapai Hill
Squaw Tank
Keys View, 5185'
Pleasant Valley
sketch x
3.8
15.2
(road impassable in wet weather)
HAPPY VALLEY
Dillon Road
road unmarked
6.2
Fargo Canyon Rd.
10
Landfill Rd.
take Dillon turnoff from I10
INDIO 3

The old ore wagon road to Daggett

Pink desert mountains glow in the distance as I cross a flat desert plain. I'm now traveling on Camp Rock Road, used to haul ore to Lucerne Valley or Daggett in the early days of mining. At dry Anderson Lake motor bikes are scouring up clouds of dust, and at so-called "Rimbender Camp" motor homes are arranged in a circle, like Conestoga wagons of pioneer days.
But the desert is vast and all this is forgotten in the appreciation of the purple, chocolate, and salmon-colored splendor of mountains lit by the morning sun. The desert floor is the warm olive hue of a hundred thousand creosote bushes. Coming out of the final canyon pass, I view the Calico Mountains, aptly named because of the many colors painting its peaks and canyons.

View of Ord Mountains from Camp Rock Road on the way to Daggett, San Bernardino County

One wagon road to Daggett

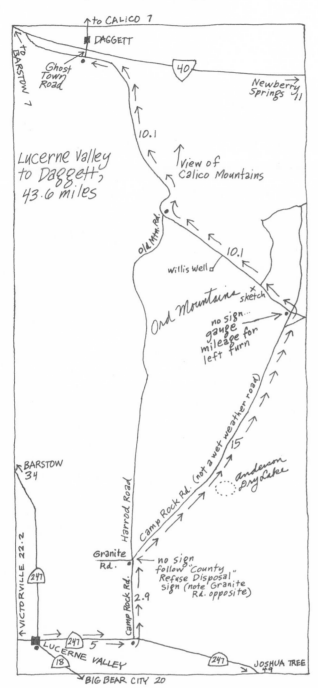

to CALICO 7

DAGGETT

to BARSTOW 7

Ghost Town Road

40

Newberry Springs 11

10.1

View of Calico Mountains

Lucerne Valley to Daggett, 43.6 miles

Old Mtn. Rd.

10.1

willis Well

Ord Mountains

sketch

no sign... gauge mileage for left turn

BARSTOW 34

Camp Rock Rd. (not a wet weather road)

15

anderson Dry Lake

Harrod Road

VICTORVILLE 22.2

247

Granite Rd.

Camp Rock Rd.

no sign follow "County Refuse Disposal" sign (note Granite Rd. opposite)

2.9

247

5

Camp Rock Rd.

LUCERNE VALLEY

18

247

JOSHUA TREE 49

BIG BEAR CITY 20

Road to Rainbow Basin

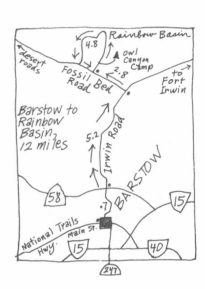

Rainbow Basin

4.8

Owl Canyon Camp

2.8

desert roads

Fossil Bed Road

to Fort Irwin

Barstow to Rainbow Basin, 12 miles

5.2

Irwin Road

BARSTOW

58

.7

15

National Trails Hwy.

Main St.

15

40

247

The road to Rainbow Basin

Near Barstow is Rainbow Basin Natural Area. It is a region of uplifted lake beds showing striated and patterned earth. There are variations of purple, beige, chocolate, gray, and green colors in the landscape.

The road winds through Rainbow Basin, giving good opportunities for viewing this unusual area.

Rainbow Basin landscape near Barstow, San Bernardino County

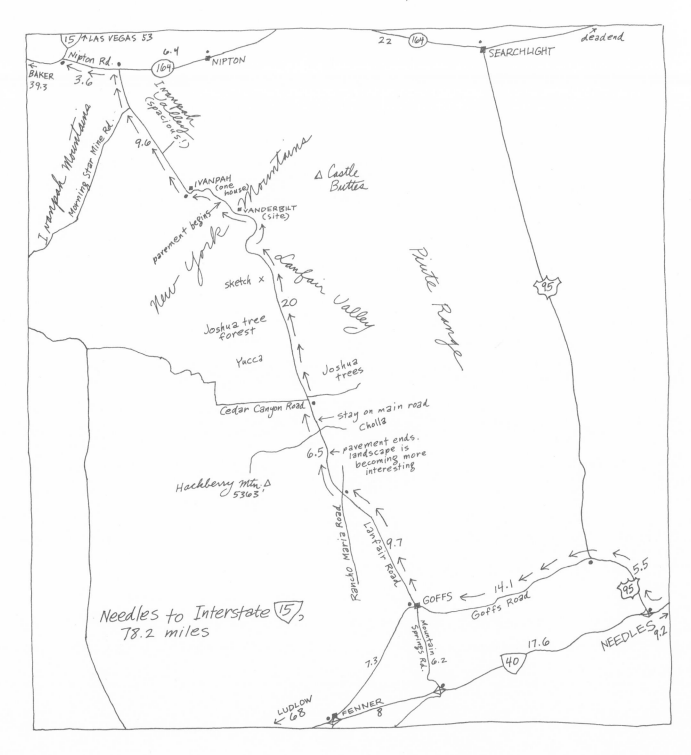

The road to Ivanpah

15 ↑LAS VEGAS 53   22 164   deadend↗
  Nipton Rd. 6.4   SEARCHLIGHT
BAKER   3.6   164   •NIPTON
39.3

Ivanpah Mountains
Morning Star Mine Rd.
Ivanpah Valley (spacious!)
9.6

■IVANPAH (one house)
pavement begins→ ■VANDERBILT (site)

New York Mountains

△ Castle Buttes

Piute Range

95

sketch ×
Lanfair Valley
20

Joshua tree forest

Yucca

Joshua trees

Cedar Canyon Road • ←stay on main road Cholla
6.5 ←pavement ends. landscape is becoming more interesting

Hackberry Mtn. △
5363'

Rancho Maria Road

Lanfair Road 9.7

5.5

14.1 ←
GOFFS ←   Goffs Road   95

Needles to Interstate 15,
78.2 miles

Mountain Springs Rd. 6.2
7.3   17.6   NEEDLES 9.2→
                40

LUDLOW   •FENNER
←68   8

183

View of the New York Mountains,
Lanfair Valley, San Bernardino
County

The road to Ivanpah (map, page 183)

    The desert road becomes more interesting as altitude increases. Mojave yuccas and joshua trees are abundant. There are close views of Piute Range and Castle Mountains across Lanfair Valley.
    I sketch the New York Mountains, orange and tan, with mountain juniper dotting them green. The sky just above the peaks is intensely blue. It is quiet here, and I muse how few chances I have to enjoy such profound stillness. When I reach Ivanpah I find but one house near the railroad tracks, with miles and miles of desert silence all around.

Back road to Cima (map, page 186)

    I see yuccas and joshuas, forests of them, as I drive toward Cima. And chollas' spiky needles glistening in the sunshine. Range cattle with immense horns sometimes block the road.
    The low elevation of the winter sun makes deep shadows in the mountains. I pass through an area forested with juniper, the pinyon pine, then joshua trees again. It is a drive with a rich variety of desert plants to observe.

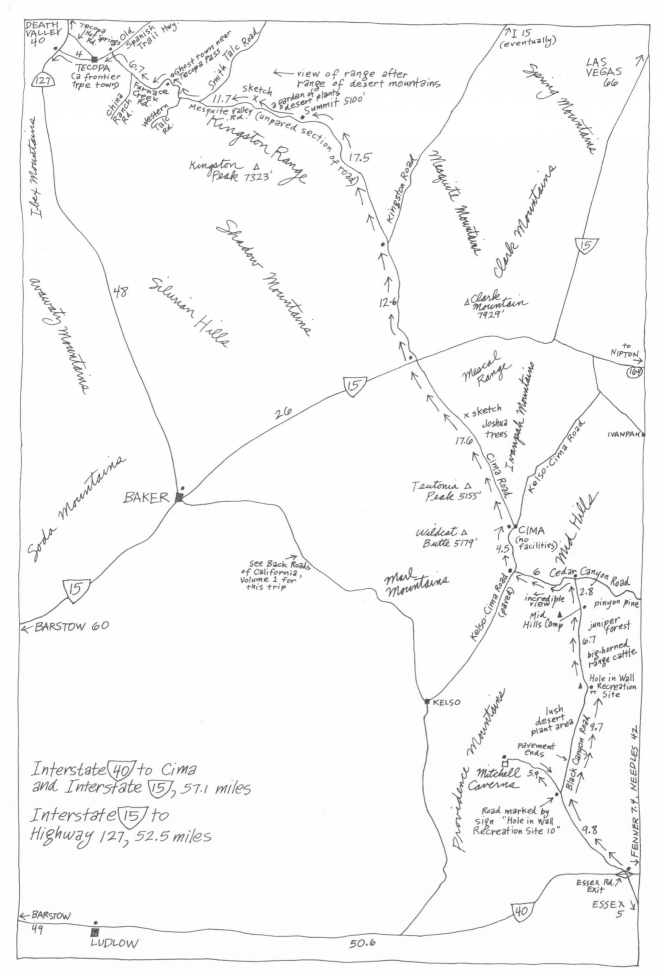

DEATH VALLEY 40

↑ Tecopa Hot Springs Rd.

Old Spanish Trail Hwy.

127

4

TECOPA (a frontier type town)

6.7

China Ranch Rd.

Furnace Creek Rd.

Western Talc Rd.

Ghost town near Tecopa Pass

Smith Talc Road

11.7

sketch x

← view of range after range of desert mountains

Mesquite Valley Rd. (unpaved section of road)

a garden of desert plants

Summit 5100'

17.5

↑I 15 (eventually)

LAS VEGAS 66

Spring Mountains

15

Kingston Range

Kingston Peak 7323'

Kingston Road

Mesquite Mountains

Clark Mountains

Ibex Mountains

Shadow Mountains

Silurian Hills

48

12.6

Clark Mountain 7929'

to NIPTON

164

IVANPAH

Mescal Range

15

26

17.6

x sketch Joshua trees

Cima Road

Ivanpah Mountains

Kelso-Cima Road

Avawatz Mountains

Soda Mountains

BAKER

Teutonia Peak 5155'

Wildcat Butte 5179'

CIMA (no facilities)

4.5

Mid Hills

15

← BARSTOW 60

See Back Roads of California, Volume 1 for this trip

Marl Mountains

Kelso-Cima Road (paved)

6

Cedar Canyon Road

incredible view!

2.8

pinyon pine

Mid Hills Camp

juniper forest

6.7

big-horned range cattle

Hole in Wall Recreation Site

KELSO

Providence Mountains

lush desert plant area

Black Canyon Road

9.7

pavement ends

Mitchell Caverns

5.9

Road marked by sign "Hole in Wall Recreation Site 10"

9.8

FENNER 7.4, NEEDLES 42

Interstate 40 to Cima and Interstate 15, 57.1 miles

Interstate 15 to Highway 127, 52.5 miles

← BARSTOW 49

LUDLOW

50.6

40

Essex Rd. Exit

ESSEX 5

Joshua trees
near Cima,
San Bernardino
County

187

Excelsior Mine Road
(map, page 186)

There is a good view of the Kingston Range as I approach the summit. At 5,100 feet, I pass through a region of heavy mining activity. At one point I wend my way through mine tailings.

Barrel cactus and cholla, near Tecopa Pass, San Bernardino County

I notice garden-like arrangements of cactus and other desert plants growing on the rocky mountainside and choose barrel cactus and cholla to draw.

The road from here descends into a vast desert valley. I pass a ghost town at Tacopa Pass and later pass the frontier-like town of Tacopa before reaching Highway 127.

Epilogue

Picturesque, old-fashioned back roads are in danger of disappearing entirely. They are threatened even in remote and sparsely populated areas of the United States. Like paths, these roads once followed the contours of the land. In fact, many of the roads followed early Indian and pioneer trails.

Today massive machines carve and redistribute the earth to achieve as direct and straight a route as possible. We have all seen road-cuts along our speed-oriented highways. They look to me like ugly wounds that have been inflicted upon the earth. I agree that we must have high-speed freeways and secondary roads; what I object to is the road-building philosophy that _all_ roads are candidates for reconstruction. And from a practical standpoint (as a taxpayer), I am concerned about the increasing costs of road building and maintenance, as more and more widening, cutting, and paving takes place. It is possible that, in many instances, grading the gravel and dirt roads and smoothing the asphalt ones are all that is really necessary.

I don't believe that a straight road is necessarily a safe one. It seems to me that a direct route encourages speed and thus increases the potential for danger.

Arriving at the destination has always been only part of my purpose. It is equally important to me to enjoy the journey itself. (It is _my_ life that is passing by, and I do not wish to waste it peering at freeway asphalt, cars, trucks, and recreational vehicles.)

The price we pay for speed is too high. I feel it is time to slow down, or at least not to increase the pace, especially on back roads.

I have investigated and catalogued back roads in eleven states. My travels have been exhilarating and have given me a great deal of joy. They have left me with a profound concern for the future of the beautiful back roads of America.

189

Index

Page numbers in italics indicate maps.

Graffiti, Donner Lake Road, Nevada County

Note: Anyone noticing discrepancies in the maps
or anyone aware of further changes is encouraged
to write to the author at:

19210 Highway 128,
Calistoga, California
94515

Materials used by the author
for the making of this book
were smooth- or rough-surfaced
Fabriano watercolor paper,
rapidograph 00 pen with
Osmiroid ink, bamboo pen
with India ink, Winsor &
Newton series 233 brushes
and Grumbacher 4701
Erminette brushes.

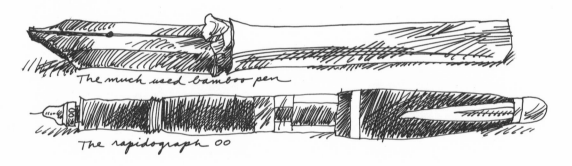

The much used bamboo pen

The rapidograph 00

Historic Spots in California,
published by Stanford University
Press, was of great help in
the author's research.

Book design, drawings, maps,
and calligraphy by Earl Thollander